BITING TALK

My Autobiography

BITING TALK

My Autobiography

NORMAN HUNTER

with Don Warters

Hodder & Stoughton

First published in Great Britain in 2004
by Hodder and Stoughton
A division of Hodder Headline

A Hodder & Stoughton Book

1 3 5 7 9 10 8 6 4 2

A CIP catalogue record for this title
is available from the British Library

ISBN 0 340 83082 4

Typeset in Plantin Light by Palimpsest Book Production,
Polmont, Stirlingshire

Printed and bound by
Clays Ltd, St Ives plc

Hodder Headline's policy is to use papers that are
natural, renewable and recyclable products and made from
wood grown in sustainable forests. The logging and
manufacturing processes are expected to conform to the
environmental regulations of the country of origin

Hodder and Stoughton Ltd
A division of Hodder Headline
338 Euston Road
London NW1 3BH

To
Sue, Michael and Claire

CONTENTS

ACKNOWLEDGEMENTS

I would like to thank my good friend Don Warters for all his help in the preparation of this book. I told the story in my own words, but Don shaped it so that the book accurately reflected my thoughts and feelings. I would like to thank the team at Hodder and Stoughton, who have encouraged me right from the beginning and who have made the publishing experience most enjoyable.

Photographic Acknowledgements

The author and publisher would like to thank the following for permission to reproduce photographs:

Associated Press, BBC Radio Leeds, Colorsport, Mirrirpix, Popperfoto.com, Press Association, Mark Swinford Photography, TopFoto, Varley Picture Agency, Yorkshire Post Newspapers Ltd.

All other photographs are from private collections.

FOREWORD
by Eddie Gray

NORMAN Hunter's hard and uncompromising tackling and his fierce determination made him one of the greatest love-hate figures in post-war British football history, but he was hard in the proper sense of football. He would make tackles, scrap and battle with opponents but it was all done in the right manner. He just wanted to be a winner and be the best.

Even in training and five-a-side matches he had this burning desire to win. When you played against him, he would kick you and smile so apologetically afterwards that somehow you didn't feel so bad about it.

A lot of people don't realise what a good footballer Norman really was. In my view, he was very underrated. I would say that, of his generation, he was probably the best club defender there was in his position. He wasn't a better international player than Bobby Moore – Moore was one of the best international players I have ever seen – but as a club player, I thought Norman was the most consistent. His standards never varied. He had remarkable stamina and fitness and he turned in top-class displays week-in and week-out.

It isn't difficult to see why he was such a popular figure with supporters but Norman didn't have it easy. He wasn't the most naturally gifted player and he needed to work hard at his game but, to me, he typifies someone who loved football and was determined to become a top player. He simply oozed enthusiasm for the game. No one got more out of their ability than Norman did out of his. He wanted to be as good as he possibly could be – and he was. He wanted to be the best and he was the best. If young players of today could have seen him play and been aware of the great determination he had, he would, in my view, have been a great example for them.

Norman loved to train because he wanted to learn all the time. I don't think he felt you could ever stop learning about the game, and he was right. His enthusiasm rubbed off on other people. There were a lot of great players in the Leeds team during the Don Revie era but, consistently, he was right up there with the best of them and it was a privilege for me to have been in the same side as him.

When he was young, I imagine there were people who thought he would never make the grade. It was a masterstroke on the part of Don Revie to switch him to centre-back and play him alongside Jack Charlton. By his own admission Norman wasn't the quickest but not many forwards got past him. He had a great knack of getting across attackers and stopping them moving into positions where they might have been able to expose his lack of pace. That was one of his greatest strengths.

When Norman finished playing, I think he could look back over an illustrious career and feel he gave it everything he had. That sums him up perfectly.

Eddie Gray

1

RED WELLIES, GAS LAMPS AND THE KING'S SEAT

To SAY I was football crazy as a youngster is putting it mildly. In my young days every lad, certainly in the north east, which was a hotbed of football talent, wanted to play football, either for Newcastle United or Sunderland. In my case, it was definitely Newcastle. I would willingly have crawled on my hands and knees the six or so miles from my home in Eighton Banks to get to St James' Park to play for the Magpies. That's how desperate I was.

Whereas all my mates played football in the streets and on the local fields, I was a bit different because I used to eat, sleep and drink football. Right from the very first time I can remember anything, I wanted to play the game that meant so much to so many people in the north east. I've no idea why that was but for me nothing else seemed to matter. As far as I was concerned, football came first, second and third on my agenda. There wasn't another choice.

I suppose you could say that living with several uncles who all played football and were ardent supporters of Newcastle

United meant that I was born into it. If that is the case, I regard myself as having been very fortunate. Football can kick you in the teeth at times but I wouldn't have changed my career for anything else. It has brought me endless hours of pleasure, fame and, I have to admit, some notoriety as well. It has also given me a great deal of satisfaction and a good standard of living, and has enabled me to make a great many friends. My playing days are long since over and I'm no longer involved in the coaching or management side of the game but the next best thing for me is talking about it and I do a lot of that in my role as a match summariser for BBC Radio Leeds and also at sporting dinners up and down the country.

All this seems a million miles away from my humble beginnings. My father, after whom I was named, died a couple of months before I was born in October 1943, and I never took it upon myself to find out much about him. I'm told he was a footballer and I believe that he played for a time with Sheffield United. He had been married before and was quite a bit older than my mother, Betty. He had retired from football and had let his fitness go quite a bit. Apparently, he was overweight when he was persuaded to make a comeback and it was while preparing for this that he suffered a heart attack and collapsed and died at a training session. At the age of twenty-one my mother was left with the task of bringing up not just me but also my brother Robert, who is eighteen months older than I am.

The three of us lived in a terraced house – number 8 Rosemary Gardens, Eighton Banks, near Wrekenton – with my mum's sister, Jean, and two of my uncles, Bill and Frank. The house had four bedrooms and we all fitted in and did the best we could. My uncles worked down the mines but, frankly, we didn't have two halfpennies to scratch our backsides with and struggled to make ends meet. My mother did what she could, working part time doing ironing, washing and even wallpapering for neighbours. But for all that we didn't have any money to speak of, they were great times for me. I thoroughly enjoyed my childhood. We made our own entertainment and in my case that meant playing football, and cricket, too, in the summer. We all made the best of the situation and we had some great laughs. They were happy days and I still enjoy a chinwag about those times whenever I meet up with old friends.

Although I didn't have a father, it was not a problem. My uncles were like fathers to me. My mother was nineteen when she had my brother, a very young age to have a child in those days, and when I appeared on the scene it was a real struggle to survive financially. There was just no money. I remember it was three old pence (roughly 1p) to get into the swimming baths and, on rare occasions, we were given the entrance money, but nothing to pay for the bus ride to get there. We didn't ask for any more because we knew we wouldn't get it. We thought ourselves lucky to get what we had been given. The baths were miles away from where we lived but we walked there and then back again. If we hadn't, we wouldn't have been able to go swimming. It was as simple as that.

If we managed to get sixpence – and that wasn't very often – we thought we had struck it rich if only for a day. A return ticket on the bus cost a penny and a halfpenny, which meant there was a bit left over to buy sweets. It was a rare treat but appreciated all the more. When money is so difficult to come by, you value it much more.

As the younger son, I used to get Robert's hand-me-down clothes. Some of them weren't new when he got them but had been passed on by friends and neighbours. There were no Nike, Umbro or other designer clothes for us. If such things existed in those days, news of them hadn't reached Eighton Banks, which was probably as well because no one would have been able to afford them anyway. The fashion in those days was for kids to play out wearing Wellington boots, and I think that was mainly because they were cheaper to buy than shoes. All my mates had black wellies. Much to my embarrassment, mine were red, same as the girls wore, hand-me-downs someone had given to my mum. That memory is still vivid in my mind. I can look back and laugh about it now but, as you can imagine, it wasn't so funny at the time. Kids can be very cruel and I had to suffer a lot of stick from my mates about those red wellies but I never got into any fights over them because I was so small in those days. Had I got into any scraps I would have come off the worst.

Being small for my age brought some problems for me as a kid but I had Rob to fight my battles. Our kid, as I used to call him, would sort them out for me. People who watched me play professional football, when I feared no one and could dish out the rough stuff with the best of them if it was needed, will probably have a wry smile at that but when you're a kid – and a small one – size does matter! These days I don't see a lot of Rob. He lives in Wickham, near Gateshead, while I live in Leeds, but when we were kids we were very close. In fact we were a tightly knit family. There was a great bond between us all and if we were to meet up right now we would just carry on as we used to. The bond is still there. We went through a lot together as youngsters and those are memories that you just never forget.

Television had not reached the masses when I was young. It was another luxury that most of us could not afford. However,

Mrs Boyle, who lived just down the road from us, had a television set and, needless to say, she was a very popular woman. We used to run errands for her and ask her if she wanted any gardening doing in the hope that she might invite us in to watch her telly. Otherwise, we had to make do with listening to the wireless. There was one programme in particular that I was hooked on – 'Dick Barton, Special Agent', which was broadcast every evening during the week from 6.45 to 7. For me, it was a programme not to be missed. The adventures of Dick Barton and his mates Jock and Snowy held me spellbound. My mum used this programme as a way of getting me to come in at night. When she called out, I would plead with her to let me stay out longer to play football. 'If you don't come in now you'll miss Dick Barton,' she would reply. It worked every time. The final whistle had blown on football for that day.

All the local kids used to play football when I was a youngster – there was very little else that you could do but as the people in the north east were so passionate about football, it was natural to play the game anyway. We played in the streets, of course, and we had our own floodlights. In those days, the streets were lit by gas lamps and we knew how to turn them on. They were set to light up at certain times but we discovered how to trip the timing gear, so when we needed them earlier, one of us would shimmy up the lampposts and switch them on.

For goals we would use the small gates of the houses, which were in a semi-circle with a gas lamp right in the middle. Each of us had a gate to defend but you also had to try to score a goal for yourself by hitting one of the gates that were being defended by your mates. They would try to do the same. Everybody played against each other but once you let in three goals that was it. You were out. If you hadn't conceded any goals after a while and the others had let in one or two, they would gang up on you and all attack your gate. I didn't realise it at the time but I was developing defensive skills that were later to play such an important part in my becoming a professional footballer. You certainly had to have your wits about you. There was plenty of action and we all got stuck in. We played that game for hours and hours until we were called in.

Kids get up to all sorts of things and we were no exception. Having been told on one occasion by an older boy that jackdaws could be trained to talk, a few of us decided to try to catch one and train it. There was a nest near where we lived, or so we had been told. It was on a ledge halfway down a cliff, so we found a rope, put it under little Eric Moody's arms and tied it around his waist. He was the youngest and smallest in the group, and the lightest. The rest of us slowly lowered him down the cliff, but just at that moment, Mum appeared, some distance away, and called out to us. 'Hello Mum,' we called back, doing our utmost to hold on to the rope while hiding it from view. Fortunately, the rope held and little Eric came to no harm but the mission failed because when he got to the nest it was empty. So we never did find out whether jackdaws could talk.

Youngsters see no danger. It's only when I cast my mind back now that I realise just how dangerous some of the things we did actually were. We were having a great time and that was all we thought about, and why not? It wasn't time for us to make our way in the big wide world. We lived in a world of our own and we loved it.

One thing got to me, though, and that was the trial of the King's Seat. You had to climb up the face of a nearby high rock and chalk your initials on the flat top, which resembled a seat. If you were too scared to do it, you were a nobody. You were allowed to join the gang only if you had chalked your initials on the top of that rock. I tried numerous times without success – I wasn't scared, it was just that I was too small – until one day I made it to the top and did the deed. What a great feeling of achievement that was! But it faded rapidly when I found I couldn't climb back down. I made it halfway then got the shakes. I was terrified and had to stay put for a long time because I was too scared to move. Eventually, I made it down by myself and was accepted into the gang.

It was always in my mind to be a footballer despite being ridiculed at school for it. Whenever the teacher went round the class asking us what we wanted to do for a living I would always reply that I wanted to be a footballer. The other kids would laugh out loud at me but I didn't care. A footballer I wanted to be and a footballer I was determined to become. No one was going to sway me from that.

I attended a tiny primary school in Eighton Banks. Four of us sat the old 11-plus examination and we all failed, so it was Birtley Secondary Modern School for us. I was hopeless there as well, except for sport, although faults were found with that, too. My old physical education teacher, who was in charge of the school football team and whose name I can't for the life of me remember, used to say to me, 'Hunter, you must learn to kick the ball with your right foot.' He came up with the bright idea for me to wear a plimsoll on my left foot rather than a football boot, so that every time I kicked the ball with my left foot it would hurt and I would try to use my right foot more to avoid the pain.

It didn't work and my other sports master, Mr Shields, told me to forget it. 'Just carry on playing with your left foot and the right foot will come good in time,' he said, but it never did. At least Mr Shields used to encourage me. He would say to me, 'Hunter, you will get there, you'll make it,' and he was right.

There was never anything else I thought about doing and as things turned out I'm glad there wasn't. I had a great time as a professional and if I had my time over again, I'd do exactly the same thing. You have to work very hard, of course, and take a lot of knocks on the way but if you're as keen as I was, it's a labour of love. Certainly it's much better than working a lathe.

I didn't make star status as a schoolboy. In fact, apart from one appearance for the Chester-le-Street district boys' team, schoolboy honours eluded me. The big lads were preferred for the schoolboy county sides and so they had the edge over us smaller kids. I had trials and did well in them – you know when you have played well and anyway, the guy who got me the trials told me so. I couldn't run past the big lads but I could knock the ball by them and get it back. My mentor warned me that my size would count against me.

At that age it never occurred to me that I was a better all-round player than the bigger lads but I thought I had better skills. As you get older, skills become even more important. Strength and size are not enough. I was never the quickest but I could always control the ball well and pass it, and my first touch was also good – which is a vital asset.

I wasn't the brightest button on the blazer, so while it was disappointing to leave school without having gained a single qualification, it was not surprising. It was fair comment to say that it was because my only real interest was football.

I've been a competitor all my life. When I was young I was taught that the game was one of physical contact and that if you were a defender your job was to win the ball, not at all costs but almost, and certainly by putting everything into a tackle. A defender who doesn't put everything he has into every tackle shouldn't be in the team. That kind of thinking earned me a 'hard man' reputation and in my early days of first-team football with Leeds I did step out of line on occasions but when I played football it had to be all or nothing. Whatever happened I gave it my all – I was very much a 100 per cent man. The battles are there in every walk of life and if you are going to be successful, you have to try to win them.

The first big challenge I won was securing a job as an electrical fitter with Henley's Cables in Birtley. There was just one vacancy and about eight of us from the same school all went for it. In those days, you had to get a job as soon as you left school, if you could. Money had to be earned and as soon as possible. With my educational background, though, I honestly thought it was a waste of time turning up for the interview. I didn't think I stood a chance of getting it. I was hardly brimming with confidence, so it was much to my amazement that I got the job. The interviewer asked me what I wanted to do and I said I would do anything to get the job. He told me afterwards that my willingness to do anything had swung it against the other lads, some of whom were better qualified.

It wasn't long before I realised my mistake in appearing to be so willing because I very quickly became the 'gofer'. The blokes I worked with used to order me to go for this, that and the other. My role, when I wasn't working my lathe, was that of general dogsbody and butt of jokes. Once I was told to go and fetch a bucket of steam, another time it was a left-handed screwdriver, and being young and naïve, I actually went looking for them! How daft can you be? But that was the kind of thing young lads who were just starting out in a job, especially in factories, had to put up with. It was a sort of tradition, I suppose, and it gave those workers who were more experienced a bit of light relief from the repetitive nature of the work. I had led a very sheltered life and as a result I was hardly worldly-wise. Being new to the job, I fell for their tricks hook, line and sinker.

At least I had a job and was earning money. My weekly pay was £2 5s 8d (about £2.29p).

People have a habit of saying you never know what lies around the corner or what life has in store for you and as I stood at my lathe churning out those little bolts, hour after hour, day in, day out, I had no idea that my life was about to undergo a major change. Very soon I was to find myself invited to Elland Road for a trial. There's another saying that it's better to be born lucky than rich. I certainly wasn't born into money and I have to admit that I felt very fortunate to be approached by Leeds United.

When the trial invite came I had played just a couple of games for a local side, Birtley Juniors, after recovering from a broken ankle, which I'd suffered in a kick-about in the street with some of my mates. I was fifteen at the time and had just left school. The talent scout must have seen something in me in those games for Birtley Juniors because he asked me to go to Elland Road so that their coaches could see what potential I might have.

The trial game with Leeds United juniors was against Bradford Park Avenue and I was selected to play at inside-right to a lad called Ronnie Blackburn, and what a good player he was. At that time Ronnie was probably the star man of the junior side and I just kept giving him the ball. We won that match 6–0. The next day there was a phone call for me and I was asked if I would like to join the Leeds groundstaff. It was music to my ears.

However, when the time came to leave home I was not so sure. I was very young and not the most confident of youngsters. After plenty of second thoughts, I was on the verge of deciding not to go when my mother stepped in. Had it not been for her encouragement I would have forfeited the chance Leeds had offered me.

Of course, there was still a long way to go if I was to taste the kind of fame that my boyhood hero, Jackie Milburn, had enjoyed during his memorable career with Newcastle, but I had taken the first step – and I had the last laugh on those classmates of mine who used to ridicule me whenever I stood up and, in answer to the teacher, proudly told everyone that I was going to be a footballer. Hunter, the scrawny kid from Eighton Banks, was on his way. The world was at my feet, literally, and nothing was going to stop me now – or so I thought.

2

SCREWDRIVERS, SWEEPING BRUSHES AND LITTLE BILLY

MY RATHER shaky bravado lasted as far as the station but didn't survive the train ride. In fact, I wasn't at all sure Mum had given me the greatest piece of advice as I boarded the train that would take me to Leeds to begin my bid for football stardom. I wished I could have stayed at home. I was a very lonely fifteen-year-old as I sat on the train wondering why I had agreed to leave. I was a bit of a home bird. Rob was the same. We were all very happy at home. We had a good laugh and enjoyed ourselves.

The train from Newcastle was two hours late arriving because of some mechanical failure or other – yes, it happened in those days, too – and it was 10.30 at night when I finally got off at Leeds City station. I wasn't too happy because I was hardly what you would call a well-travelled young lad. Apart from a few days' holiday in Whitley Bay, the furthest I had been previously was a bus or tram ride to Newcastle or a day trip to Durham. Most of my school holidays were spent playing football, and in the summer I would pick up a bat and play cricket, too. These were the things I was thinking about during the train journey.

Leeds didn't look too welcoming late at night but, fortunately, Billy Leighton, who had been sent to meet me, was still there. As we drove along the cobbled streets of Beeston to his mother's terraced home, I really did begin to wonder what I had let myself in for. It was not the best area in the world but, as things turned out, I could not have had better digs.

The lingering euphoria I felt at having earned a place on the groundstaff evaporated rapidly as reality set in and I quickly found my place in the scale of things. It didn't take a genius to know that the groundstaff boys were at the very bottom of the pile. You might be a very promising player destined to grace football stadiums both here and abroad and become a valuable asset to the club, but that counted for little at this stage. It was a 'maybe' situation and at such a young age you were more use to your club as a toilet attendant, a gardener or a general maintenance boy. There were fifteen to twenty of us and, in common with all football clubs in those days, the groundstaff lads were used as a form of cheap labour.

Settling into digs was the first hurdle and although I was terribly homesick at first, Ma Leighton, as we all called her, did her best to make me feel at home in my new surroundings. Every six weeks we were allowed to go home for a few days and I couldn't wait for my first break. Once the junior match was over on that particular Saturday, off I went back to the north east as fast as I could. Eventually, I got into the swing of things and was not as desperate to go home. I realised that if I was going to make it as a professional footballer, I had to make my own way in life, so I got a grip on myself.

Living at Ma Leighton's when I arrived was her other son, Tony, who was also on the groundstaff at Leeds, a Welsh boy called Terry Casey, an Irish boy whose name I cannot remember, and a Scottish lad by the name of Billy Bremner. Tony signed professional forms for Leeds but never made a league appearance for the club. He enjoyed a successful career in the game as a centre-forward with various other clubs including Huddersfield Town, Doncaster Rovers, Barnsley and Bradford City.

Billy was eighteen months older than the rest of us and not only was he a professional, he had also just broken into the reserves. In our eyes Billy was the King. The pay for young professionals at that time was £13 a week plus £5 appearance fee. That was mega money. Billy was a dapper young man, very smart, with loads of clothes. Yes, we all looked up to him, especially as he had a car. Not many working-class people had cars in those days – back home in Eighton Banks we never even dreamed of owning one – and here was a young footballer, not all that much older than I was, who drove a car. He never had to think about washing and polishing it because we were only too eager to do it for him. He didn't pay us, of course, but that didn't bother us. We did it so that he would give us a ride in it!

Had it not been for Ma Leighton and the way she looked after me, I would not have stuck it out at Leeds in those early months. I will always be grateful to her. She was superb. She did all the washing, loading all our clothes into a pram and pushing it to the laundry. On Sundays, her husband, Cornelius, would use the pram to deliver newspapers around the Beeston area. Cornelius – everyone called him Con – never liked me. I don't know why or if I had done anything to upset him, but he just didn't take to me. The old fella was jealous as hell of Billy. 'You treat him better than you treat me,' he used to say to his wife, but it made no difference. Billy was clearly Ma Leighton's favourite and she would always have chocolate biscuits waiting for him when he came in.

Billy was a shining example to me of what was possible if you were good enough and lucky enough to earn a professional contract. But he might well have been lost to Leeds United because he also had suffered terribly from homesickness when he first arrived from Scotland. It got so bad that at one stage he decided he'd had enough, packed his bags and went back to his hometown of Stirling. He had a girlfriend, Vicki, back in Stirling and it took a lot of sweet-talking by someone from the Leeds club to persuade him to come back, and even then he still had thoughts of returning north of the border before the call came for him to make his debut in the reserves. He married Vicki when he was very young – nineteen I think – and went on the transfer list. Thankfully, no club came up with a successful bid for him and the wee fella eventually, of course, became one of the Elland Road club's all-time great players.

Our experience as young players was very different from the way promising young players of today are treated. Now they get the best of everything and I've no complaints about that. It's right and proper for clubs to give youngsters the best possible chance of realising their potential. It makes sense for clubs to develop their own stars. But I thought I had it good back in the sixties. After all, I had gone from earning £2 5s 8d a week, working a lathe, to picking up £8 as a groundstaff boy with a professional football club. Out of that I had to pay for my digs and I used to send about £5 a month back home to my mum, but I had something left in my pocket for myself. I felt as though the world was at my feet. I had got over my homesickness and I loved the whole thing – playing football, living in digs with other lads and the general ambience of the situation.

I used to love training and took a lot of stick from the other lads about that. They thought I was crackers, but I really couldn't wait to get out there on the training pitch. For me, it was brilliant.

Training back in those days was not what it is now. I heard the stories about players being told to train by running up Morley Hill, which is not far from Elland Road, and some of them stopping off at a pub halfway up before catching a bus back to the ground, having splashed some water over their faces to try to look suitably sweaty and tired when they got back. I don't know if they were true but training, shall we say, did leave a bit to be desired.

In fact, one of my earliest memories of life at Elland Road concerns an attempt to upgrade the club's training methods. Willis Edwards, a former England international who was one of the best wing-halves of his day and gave Leeds United great service, was assistant trainer to Bob Roxburgh. He, Maurice Lindley, who went on to become assistant manager of the club, and Bob English, who was trainer-cum-physiotherapist, had been at pains to set up a circuit on the Elland Road pitch. They had carefully placed cones in strategic places along with mats, footballs and skipping ropes. Unfortunately for the coaching staff, some of the older lads didn't fancy circuit training one little bit. It was foreign to their nature. So they promptly gathered together all the cones and threw them down the banking at the corner of the ground.

The downside of life at the club was the menial work the groundstaff boys were expected to do. The worst job of all was cleaning the toilets on the Monday morning after a Saturday game. We'd all be there waiting for the groundsman, Cec

Burrows, to detail the jobs we would be doing that morning and every one of us hoped against hope that we wouldn't get the toilet duty. It was the one job to avoid at all costs. We all hated it. What a state the toilets were in – especially the ladies. They were absolutely shocking. How people could go in and use them I really didn't know. Sweeping the terraces was extremely boring and time consuming but immensely preferable to cleaning the toilets.

We also had to clear up the refreshment bars, look after the dressing rooms and help to maintain the pitch. They didn't use a lot of fertiliser on the playing surface, so weeds tended to thrive. The club's answer to that was to use the groundstaff lads. We were issued with screwdrivers and had to go over the pitch digging out the weeds, right down to the roots, with them. 'If you do that, they don't come back,' Cec used to say. Percy Thrower would have been proud of us! Seeing all these boys armed with screwdrivers creeping about the pitch on their hands and knees must have been quite a funny sight.

As well as being the weed-control squad, we would help re-seed the pitch in the summer months ready for a new season. Nowadays people would think we were crazy. I often wonder what some of the young lads in the academies would think if they had to do things like that. Somehow, the idea of Harry Kewell, Alan Smith, James Milner, Michael Owen or Wayne Rooney cleaning out the toilets or digging weeds out of a pitch with a screwdriver doesn't ring true, does it? They would probably pass out with shock. But I have to confess that to this day I still use a screwdriver to dig out the weeds in my lawn!

Work for the groundstaff boys began at 9 a.m. and we used to arrive early so that we could get changed and have a cup of tea with the laundry ladies. At nine o'clock sharp, we came under the charge of the groundsman. As you can imagine, with so many boys together we used to mess about a lot, but no matter what we did we had to finish the jobs we were given to Cec's satisfaction before we were allowed to train. You could say that weeding the pitch was more important than training. Although there was no shirking, it was usually 2.30 or three o'clock by the time we had finished our jobs.

We used to clean boots, of course, and we would sort out the kit but we were not allowed into the first-team dressing room. In fact, we were frightened to death of the first-team players. Very occasionally we would get the chance to play in a practice game. The call would come, 'The reserves are one short,' and every one of us would volunteer to fill that place. When I was chosen I was off like a shot. Apart from anything else, it got you out of your work detail. But there was a big barrier between the first team and the groundstaff lads. I've no idea why but that was the way it was in those days. First-team players were a level above you. They knew it and you knew it, and if you didn't, you were soon reminded about it. My old adversaries Tommy Smith and Nobby Stiles, two of the most aggressive players of their era, tell me they had to endure that kind of thing when they were young lads at Liverpool and Manchester United, seeking to make their way in professional football. You were just not allowed to mix with the first-team players.

If I had to go to the dressing room for any reason, I dreaded it. You had to knock on the door before you went in, and if one or two of them weren't in the right mood, they would clip you across the ear and chuck you out – no messing. We all tried our best not to upset Jack Charlton, John McCole, a Glaswegian who played centre-forward, Noel Peyton, Grenville Hair and most of the others. Later I came to realise there were some right characters among those players, including McCole. 'Call me King – King McCole,' he used to say to the groundstaff lads. He could play a bit – he scored over 50 goals in 85 first-team games for Leeds United, who bought him from Bradford City for £10,000 after he had scored 32 goals in his first season for them.

No one ever clipped me around the ears but I knew my place just as the rest of the young lads did – and if it had happened to me, I would have accepted it just as they did. It was the way things were at football clubs back in those days. Football was a tough environment for a teenager. You had to be strong to survive and those who weren't often fell by the wayside. You also had to be thick-skinned. I was so small and puny that as a joke the lads nicknamed me Tarzan! It's funny how nicknames tend to stay with you – to this day Mick Bates, whenever he sees me, greets me with a cheery, 'Hi Tarz.' Billy Bremner became known as Chalky after he was sent off along with Kevin Keegan in a Charity Shield match at Wembley. In a show of anger, both of them flung off their shirts as they left the pitch, Keegan to reveal a bronzed, hairy chest and Billy to show off his milky white one.

However, nicknames were the least of our worries. We had a coach on the staff at that time by the name of Syd Owen, who was later to become a member of Don Revie's famous backroom team. Birmingham-born Syd, a centre-half whose last game as a player was in Luton Town's FA Cup final against Nottingham Forest in 1959, was a difficult man to please. His standards were very high. Syd, who used to play me at outside-left in the juniors, could be very cutting with his remarks. I think he felt that the harder he came down on a young lad, the harder his 'victim' would try to prove him wrong. I remember him saying to me, 'Norman, you're not very quick, you can't head a ball, you can't run but you're first touch is all right and you can pass a ball. So just get it and knock it off to someone else who can play.' And I was one of his favourites!

If he had got on to me in the way he got on to some of the other lads, I don't think I would have survived it. Eddie Gray arrived at the club from Scotland with a big reputation, as did Peter Lorimer, and that was like a red rag to a bull for Syd. Reputations, especially at such a young age, meant nothing to him, and he frequently had a go at those two, just as he did with Terry Yorath and one or two of the other lads when they first arrived. He purposely took them down a peg or two. There was no chance of any budding young hopeful becoming too big for his boots with Syd around. He liked Paul Reaney but he wasn't too keen on Gary Sprake, and as far as Terry Cooper was concerned he could take him or leave him.

Syd was a hard taskmaster but he was a good coach and I suppose in some cases he was being cruel to be kind. A lot of the youngsters who came under his charge turned out to be great players. But I can remember that when the time came for a decision to be made on Paul Madeley, the talk around the club was that he would not be signed on either Syd's or Les Cocker's recommendation. Don Revie, who had recently become player-manager, was having none of that. 'I'm signing him,' he said. What a good decision that was.

While those were uncertain times for me, I counted myself very fortunate to be there at all. Some little time earlier I had been involved in a car smash in Elland Road, not far from the stadium. I had left Ma Leighton's by then and was living in digs in another area of Leeds – the Carr Manor estate. One night, Terry Casey and I had arranged to go out with Alan Humphreys, a goalkeeper, and the proud owner of a car. When he arrived, Casey and I raced each other in a bid to grab the front passenger seat and, needless to say as I was not the fastest runner, I lost. So I had to squeeze into the back with John Hawksby and Noel Peyton. It was foggy as we drove along Elland Road and suddenly Alan was yanking the steering wheel to the right to avoid a lorry across the road. The car skidded and slammed sideways into it. Poor Terry took the full brunt of the smash. The car just folded in on him. His injuries were so bad that he nearly died. I couldn't help thinking that had I been faster, it would have been me in that front passenger seat and me who suffered those life-threatening injuries. Casey, who had just forced his way into the reserves, eventually recovered and came back but he was never quite the same.

Former Queens Park Rangers manager Jack Taylor was manager when I first joined Leeds. He had been there for about six months and things were not going too well on the field. The team were well down the First Division and he felt it was time to call a meeting to thrash things out. It was just before Christmas, some seven or eight weeks after I arrived, and all the players were there from the first team down to the newcomers. He was a very polite man but to my surprise no one took a blind bit of notice of what he was saying. Several first-team players were throwing Christmas streamers across the room while he was talking. That's how much they cared about the manager's lecture and I just couldn't believe their attitude, especially as Leeds United had lost their top division status at the end of 1959–60 season, having finished in 21st position and lost 20 of their 42 league games.

As a junior, I didn't have a lot to do with the manager, of course, but as I approached my seventeenth birthday, the one thing on my mind was a professional contract. It was a vital time for any young footballer hoping to make it big in the game and I was no exception. At the end of the season, all the groundstaff lads gathered together in a room and waited to be summoned one by one to learn our fate. Afterwards, some were crying, having been told that they weren't good enough to be given a contract, and others were on a high, having been told the opposite. You can imagine how gutted I felt when Jack Taylor told me, 'I'm sorry, son, but I don't think you are strong enough or big enough to make it as a professional.'

I was devastated, but all was not lost because he agreed to keep me at the club until the next spring to see if I developed. That was something to hold on to. My dream had not been entirely shattered. It was on hold, in a state of limbo. As I viewed it, I'd earned a stay of execution.

Luckily for me – but not for him – before that period was up Jack Taylor got the sack and Don Revie, who had joined Leeds in the twilight of his playing career, was appointed player-manager. I didn't know it then but it proved to be a masterstroke not only for Leeds United but also for me. I was about to embark on a great adventure.

3

THE GAFFER, HIS MAGIC POTION AND MY BIG BREAK

D ON REVIE was a great manager, a terrific motivator who possessed a wealth of football knowledge, initially as a player of skill and technical ability, and later as a very successful manager, the most successful Leeds United have ever had. I have nothing but admiration for him. I will never forget what he did for me and neither will the other lads who played for him at Leeds during the 1960s and 1970s. It was Don Revie who made my dream come true when he signed me as a professional for Leeds and Don Revie who turned me into a defender although I had never thought of myself as one. They were great days, heady days, now in the dim and distant past, but they remain memorable for me and for the supporters who followed the team at that time, as I have found out on my travels around the country as an after-dinner speaker.

When Revie was appointed player-manager in March 1961, I was still sweating it out wondering if I would be taken on as a full-time professional, and he proved to be the answer to my prayers. His first signing was Albert Johanneson, the black South African winger who had come on a three-month trial, and I was his second.

The Gaffer, as we called him, had joined Leeds as a player in November 1958 from Sunderland for the princely sum of £12,000 but when he signed me on I don't think he had actually seen much of me as a player. It was probably Les Cocker and Syd Owen who put my case to him. To be honest, I didn't know too much about him, either. I knew that he had played for Sunderland and I had heard of the 'Revie Plan' without knowing what that entailed, and that was the sum total of my knowledge of him. When he signed me, though, I thought he was the bee's knees from the word go. I couldn't sign on the dotted line quickly enough. He knew I wasn't big enough or strong enough but he simply told me, 'Just carry on what you've been doing and we'll see how things turn out.'

Full-time training seemed to do the trick for me. In a short space of time I grew from being about 5ft 7ins to just short of 6ft. Suddenly I had the height but I was just like a beanpole, still very thin and weak. Sometimes after training I would feel very good but other days I would feel so lethargic, probably because I had grown so quickly. The Gaffer came up with his own solution to my problem, a special potion consisting of a glass of sherry with raw egg mixed in it. I had to swallow this concoction every day before I left home for training. It was dreadful. I hated the stuff but that made no difference to the Gaffer. He asked me every day to make sure I'd taken it. Sometimes I hadn't reached the changing rooms before he would accost me with, 'Norman, have you had your sherry and eggs?'

'Yes, Gaffer, yes,' I would reply dutifully.

I have to give him credit, though – the club supplied me with the sherry and the eggs, and not the cheap stuff, either. Revie made sure it was the best – Harvey's Bristol Cream and I suppose the eggs were free range and fresh! But whatever they were and wherever they came from, that potion tasted absolutely vile and there was the odd occasion early on when it made me throw up. I stuck with it because I wanted to improve my physique and fitness level and if this was a way of doing it, I was willing to put up with it. This went on for about eighteen months and, looking back, I suppose I'm lucky I didn't become an alcoholic!

Having signed a professional contract, I bought one of Leeds United's club houses in Wortley, only a mile or so away from the Elland Road stadium and just a couple of doors away from where our trainer, Les Cocker, lived. Mum came down to look after me. We ate well thanks to the Gaffer, who made sure that the club sent steaks and plenty of eggs, again with the intention of building me up. Steak was a rarity back home when I was growing up so to have it provided was very welcome.

The junior side I played in had some good young players – Paul Reaney, Gary Sprake and Paul Madeley, for instance, and Terry Cooper, who had initially turned up at Elland Road asking for a trial and carrying his boots in a brown paper bag. Paul Reaney was a centre-half then, Terry Cooper played on the left wing and I played inside-forward. We never won anything – strange, perhaps, considering we all went on to make it big time in football.

When I look back now it's surprising to me that so many good young players should have been on the groundstaff at the same time at a Second Division club – and a struggling one at that. It wasn't as if Leeds were the most glamorous of clubs, yet all these very talented lads arrived at more or less the same time. I have often been asked how this came about and really I think it was down to coincidence.

I could never understand how Leeds signed Peter Lorimer and Eddie Gray because every club in the country – and Scotland – wanted them. Someone at Leeds had some persuasive powers or the gift of the gab, or more likely both. Peter and Eddie must have been the best schoolboys of all time to come out of Scotland, certainly Peter was. I saw his cuttings from his schoolboy days and they were something special. Jack Charlton and Billy Bremner were already at the club. Others who followed were David Harvey, Terry Yorath, Mick Bates, Rod Belfitt, Terry Hibbitt and Jimmy Greenhoff. I doubt that you would find such a situation occurring these days. Most of the good young players are snapped up by the top few clubs.

We had to work hard, of course, but we were young and ambitious and we had such great determination to succeed. I never took anything for granted, even when I signed my first contract – far from it, in fact. I knew I had to progress and convince people that I could step up into the first team. To do that, I needed to play well in the junior side and then the reserve team.

When Revie was appointed player-manager at Leeds, there is no doubt that the club had problems. Discipline had been in a shocking state and he knew it. Syd Owen and Les Cocker had been brought in under Jack Taylor in a bid to straighten things out. Syd, who won three England caps, was a highly respected centre-half in his days with Luton Town, whom he also managed for a while before joining Leeds, and he didn't suffer fools gladly. He was a supremely fit man who lived, breathed and slept football. However a conversation with him started, it always came back to football. Les, a forward who played for Accrington Stanley and later became assistant coach at Luton, wasn't all that big but he was as tough as they come. On the face of it they were the ideal pair to put the discipline back into Leeds United but boy, did they have some problems.

Syd had more fights and arguments than Les because his attitude was 'You do it my way or not at all'. There were some right rows. Some of the older players, who had not had too much respect for Jack Taylor, had got used to doing it their own way and, faced with an unruly lot of players, Syd and Les found it difficult to get the message across – until Revie took charge.

He was only thirty-three when he became player-manager, which was very young in those days, but he knew that if he was to stand a chance of succeeding he would immediately have to lay down the law. One or two of the older players got a rude awakening when the Gaffer took over. Big Jack Charlton and John McCole liked a laugh and were, perhaps, not as disciplined as they might have been. Under Taylor, if they hadn't wanted to do something, they didn't do it. All that stopped under the Revie regime. The slate was wiped clean ready for a fresh start and it wasn't long before, with the help of Syd and Les, he began to sort things out, although he had cause to jump on one or two players. Once the discipline was back in the club, there was only one way you did things – the way you were told.

Starting from scratch, Revie had to earn the respect of established players but he had it already from the young players he brought through to the first team. He certainly had mine. The only players of note among the more experienced I can remember staying were big Jack and little Billy, the two he felt he could build a team around. He got rid of the others gradually and brought in such players as Scottish international goalkeeper Tommy Younger, a thirty-one-year-old who three years earlier had captained Scotland's 1958 World Cup squad. Tommy later went on to become a director of Scottish club Hibernian, and president of the Scottish FA. Cliff Mason, a left full-back, was signed from Sheffield United in a £10,000 deal, striker Ian Lawson came from Burnley for £20,000, Jim Storrie, another goalscorer, joined from Airdrie in a £15,000 move. These transfer fees are insignificant compared to those of the present day but Leeds were a struggling club in the 1960s and spending what were then such large amounts showed the faith the board had in their new manager.

Revie had further financial backing when he went to Everton to sign Scottish international Bobby Collins for £25,000 and what a masterstroke that turned out to be. Wee Bobby was thirty-one at the time and his arrival was not all that well received by some in Leeds, who felt he was nearing the end of his career. He had enjoyed a memorable ten-year stint with Celtic before joining Everton and there were those who questioned the wisdom of bringing him to Elland Road. The Gaffer knew what he was doing but I think even he was surprised at the massive impact Bobby had on the club.

Bobby stood just 5ft 4ins tall and weighed a little over 10st but he was a massive man in all other ways. In my book he is among the greatest players ever to have played for the club. In him we had one of the best players I have ever seen. He was an absolute cracker. He could hit short passes, long passes, tackle and score goals, and he was the bravest individual I ever came across. He had a great appetite for the game and wonderful vision. People have their own ideas of what the turning point was for Leeds back in the 1960s. Some would say the signing of Johnny Giles from Manchester United but there is no doubt in my mind that it was Revie's decision to bring Bobby to Elland Road. He came to keep us out of the Third Division and he did that and much more. He was awesome for a little fella. I have always said that you realise how good players are when they are not in the team. He suffered a few broken bones at Leeds and when he wasn't playing we certainly missed him.

Bournemouth had been keen to take Revie as their manager and the Leeds chief of the time, Harry Reynolds, a blunt speaking but very likeable down-to-earth Yorkshireman who had made his money out of scrap metal, had gone as far as writing out a reference for him. He referred to the Gaffer in glowing terms and when he read his letter through, it suddenly hit home that if he was that good, he was the ideal man to be manager of Leeds United.

Reynolds might well have had second thoughts when the Gaffer began his managerial career because it was far from an auspicious beginning. His task in his first full season, 1961–62, turned out to be to save the club from dropping into the Third Division and it proved to be a nail-biting experience. Those involved fought right to the end and managed to remain unbeaten in the last nine games of the campaign, winning 3–0 in the final match at Newcastle. While this was going on, I was striving to make my mark in the reserves.

I was playing for the juniors when Revie took me on one side for a chat. He told me that Jim Storrie had remarked what an awkward 'so and so' I was to play against. Apparently, Jim had told the Gaffer that every time he played against me I always managed to get the ball off him and that I seemed to be able to get a foot in and do this, that and the other and come away with the ball.

'In our next reserve game, I'm going to play you as a defender alongside the centre-half,' Revie said.

The centre-half happened to be a lad by the name of Tommy Hallett and the next reserve game was against Manchester United. Albert Quixall, an inside-forward with a big reputation, who had been transferred for a then British transfer record fee of £45,000 from Sheffield Wednesday, was playing for the Reds. He had been in the first team but was having a run-out with the reserves. So here I was playing at the heart of the defence for the first time and I made my mark but not really as I would have liked – we drew 2–2 and I scored an own goal. That slip up apart, I felt I did okay. The Gaffer must have thought so because from then on he kept me in defence.

Most kids of my era wanted to play at centre-forward. Scoring goals makes it a much more glamorous role and forwards always seem to get the most acclaim, but that wasn't for me. I had never had any real desire to play up front and I was never thought of as a centre-forward, probably because I was so small. I had been played at outside-left and inside-left but I instinctively used to drift back and I would find myself playing a defensive role without realising it. So thanks to Jim Storrie and Don Revie's willingness to listen and experiment, I was now a central defender. My career direction had been determined and it was up to me to make the most of it.

I made the breakthrough to the reserves towards the end of the season, with just a few games left to play, but the following campaign was only half a dozen games old when I was catapulted into the first team. That brave but startling decision by Don Revie ignited the blue touch paper and launched me on the road to soccer fame.

The seventh game of the season took place at Swansea on 8 September 1962. Rod Johnson was given his debut too, and so was Paul Reaney, while Gary Sprake made his second appearance. Rod was a good goalscorer and he marked his debut by scoring our first in a 2–0 victory. Billy Bremner got the second.

Although we'd travelled with the first-team squad we didn't think we had a prayer of playing. As far as we were concerned, we had gone along for the ride and to get some idea of what went on in the build-up to a first-team match. The first we knew of our inclusion in the side was just an hour before kick-off. The Gaffer took the four of us under the stand at the Vetch Field and dropped the bombshell that we would all be playing that afternoon. I couldn't believe it. Neither could the others. I had been working so hard for this chance but I was staggered when he told me. I was also very nervous.

Gary had made his debut towards the end of the 1961–62 season, just a few days before his seventeenth birthday, when he was flown to Southampton on the morning of the game to take over from Tommy Younger, who had fallen ill, but Paul, Rod and I had not had a sniff of the first team before. The Leeds side that day was: Sprake, Reaney, Mason, Smith, Charlton, Hunter, Peyton, Bremner, Johnson, Collins, Johanneson.

Revie took a big gamble that day, especially as three of the four he brought in were defenders – a goalkeeper, a central defender and a right full-back. He didn't explain his reasoning to us but he did tell us that he had deliberately not warned us the night before the game that we would be playing because he didn't want it to prey on our minds. He wanted us to get a good night's sleep. 'Get out there and just do what you're good at,' were his words to us as we left the dressing room.

I was very pleased he sprang it on us in the way he did. Had I been told the night before, I don't think I would have got any sleep. As it was, by the time we had got changed it was almost time for the game to kick off. The ninety minutes went very quickly. I was playing alongside Jack Charlton, who helped me through the game, and Bobby Collins also supported me.

Chelsea were our next opponents and they arrived at Elland Road as Second Division leaders. Their side included a young Terry Venables. Peter Bonetti was in goal and also on duty that day were Eddie McCreadie, Bobby Tambling and Barry Bridges. All of them went on to become internationals, Eddie with Scotland and Peter, Bobby, Terry and Barry for England. We must have done well enough at Swansea as Revie kept Paul, Gary and me in the side although Rod, who had been carried off in that match with a head injury, was out. We did the business again and ran out 2–0 winners with Albert Johanneson scoring both goals.

The decision Revie took at Swansea to use his young players paid off in the long term because it sowed the seeds for what grew into the most successful period in Leeds United's history. The Gaffer had already shown he was not afraid to take a gamble in the transfer market with Bobby Collins and despite cash being so tight at the start of the 1962–63 season, he battled hard to bring back the great John Charles from Italy.

The Gentle Giant, as he was known, had been sold by Leeds to Juventus for £65,000 in May 1957. That wasn't just a British record transfer fee. It made John the most expensive footballer in the world although that didn't stop the cynics saying he would struggle to make an impact in the defensive Italian game. But he had immense talent and strength and he proved them all wrong. He netted more than 100 goals for Juventus and became an idol in Italy during his five-year stay.

John was equally at home as a centre-forward or a centre-half. Not many attackers could beat him in the air and when he switched to play up front he responded by scoring goals as though they were going out of fashion. In one season for Leeds – 1953–54 – he totalled 42 league goals in 39 outings to set up a club record that has never been beaten. The season before he was transferred, he found the net 38 times in 40 league games. He was a phenomenal player as his overall record for Leeds shows – 153 goals in 308 league appearances. That club record stood until Peter Lorimer smashed it in the mid 1980s although Peter's aggregate goal tally of 168 league goals came from 525 appearances. The first of those 525 league outings for Peter actually came in the 1962–63 season when he was suddenly brought in for a home game against Southampton in the September of that campaign. He was only fifteen years and 289 days old – the youngest person to play for Leeds in the league – but I cannot recall much about his performance that day. It was an isolated appearance because he had to wait until the end of the 1964–65 campaign for his next taste of first-team football. He turned out to be a fantastic player, which didn't surprise me one bit because he was so talented as a youngster.

During the short time John was with Leeds in the autumn of 1962, I had the opportunity to play alongside him in defence for just half a game, against Southampton, and it is something I will never forget. It was a great pleasure and a privilege. A big, strong lad called George Kirby used to play for the Saints. He was extremely polite when he met you off the field but on it he was just the opposite – an absolute beast. In this particular game, Jack Charlton felt the full force of one of George's challenges, his elbow having made contact with Jack's nose, which was broken in the incident. No substitutes were allowed in those days, so Jack had to switch to play up front and John Charles, who had been playing there, dropped back into defence. What an experience that was for me and what a player John was! He could head a ball further than I could kick it. I remember him clashing with George Kirby. It wasn't a foul but he got up well, knocked George flying and headed the ball away.

John may have been past his best but he was still an awesome figure of a man. I remember watching him take his shirt off in the dressing room before the game and his chest seemed to go on forever. He had such huge shoulders. What a player he must have been in his prime. People say he was the best footballer there has ever been, but when he returned to Leeds he had put on some weight and the move was not really the success many had hoped it would be. He netted three goals in 11 league games. However, his reputation in Italy was such that when he left Leeds, Roma paid what was reported to be more than Leeds had paid to bring him back from Juventus.

Sadly, the Gentle Giant is no longer with us but he will never be forgotten. The esteem in which he was held was underlined by the outpouring of grief that followed his death in February 2004 at the age of seventy-two, not least in Italy where he was still revered. Although he was so powerfully built, he was a man of graciousness and humility, completely untouched by the fame he achieved as a footballer. At his funeral at Leeds Parish Church on St David's Day, which was so fitting for a Welshman, many of the sport's greatest figures were there to pay their last respects.

I was proud and privileged to be one of those who helped carry his coffin into church.

After John left us for AS Roma, we battled on and found we were starting to pick up a reputation as a hard and sometimes overly aggressive side and I suppose that we were. If any one player set the standard of how we would play it was Bobby Collins. He was as hard as nails – probably the hardest man I ever came across – and a fierce competitor. I had my eyes opened when we played Preston North End. It was my thirteenth first-team game and one I'll never forget.

Don Revie was big on preparations and he used to have dossiers compiled on all our opponents. Every little detail of how they played and what they were likely to do in any given situation was included. All their strengths and weaknesses were duly noted and everyone knew with whom he had to deal. In this game at Preston I was detailed to mark their big No. 6 at set-pieces – I didn't know his name and I never did find out – and very early on he gave Bobby a kick. Some time later they won a corner. Bobby came over to me and told me to mark his man and leave the man I should have been marking to him.

'But Bobby, the Gaffer will give me a right rollocking if I don't mark the man I'm supposed to mark,' I protested, to which he replied, 'Do as I effing tell you. Take my man and I'll take yours.'

So I did. When the ball came over from the corner, Jack Charlton got up and headed it away. Bobby leapt up, too, and launched himself with everything he had at the big No. 6, who went down as though he had been pole-axed – which I suppose in a way he had. Then Bobby was off like a shot to the halfway line. You couldn't see him for dust. I was left standing near the No. 6 sprawled out on the ground and everyone thought I'd done it. I took the blame while Bobby was inside the centre circle smirking.

When you saw someone of Bobby's size make challenges like that it set you thinking. He was a great motivator and when he shouted out during games, 'Come on, get stuck in,' believe me, you did. He set the example and it seemed to carry on from there. Bobby epitomised Leeds United. He had this great will to win and it rubbed off on the rest of us. There were players in the team who just didn't know what defeat was. Jack, for instance, wouldn't lose to any one. There was a big metal sign in our dressing room which read simply 'Keep Fighting' and that's just what we did.

I suppose it's laughable to think of Norman Hunter as anything other than a hard man and I'm the first to admit that I wasn't an angel in my playing days. As a defender, I went in for tackles as hard as I could with the intention of winning the ball. It was what I had been taught and it seemed right to me. Les Cocker taught me the lesson. We used to train on Fullerton Park, a piece of land adjacent to the Elland Road stadium with a corrugated iron fence around two sides of the playing area. Later, the club seeded it but initially the surface was shale. Les Cocker would play in the practice games and he used to clatter into you, sending you sprawling. Often, you would end up hitting the fencing. I think it was his way of trying to toughen us up. On one occasion, shortly after I had made it into the first team, the ball dropped between Les and me soon after the kick-off. I thought, right mate, this is payback time. I charged in and hit him with everything I had. I put him into the air and into the fencing. I wondered what I had let myself in for but Les looked up at me with a huge smile, as if to say, 'Great, you've learnt, you've got the idea now.' Then he turned to John Hawksby and gave him the biggest rollocking of his young life for not having passed the ball to him more accurately!

As far as Les was concerned, Norman Hunter had finally arrived and I suppose I had, but I have to confess that despite the macho image, I was always the nervous type. I was very nervous when I made my first-team debut and I was nervous throughout my career. In a way, I don't think that was such a bad thing. The only way I could do it was to be psyched up for every game. Sometimes I was too psyched up and Johnny Giles would come up to me and tell me to calm down. Other players handled things differently. Peter Lorimer, for example, was never nervous. Gary Sprake was, to the point that he was physically sick before games. Paul Reaney and Paul Madeley never seemed to be affected by nerves but I think they were in their own way. Billy took everything in his stride. He was never bothered but he was such a gifted player. Jack was different. He frequently assumed an air of authority and bossed everyone around, but he had been a player when we were on the groundstaff in the days when the two sections did not mix – a bit of a throwback to the previous regime you could say.

Jack always looked after me, though, perhaps because I was a fellow Geordie. Playing alongside him, as I did for quite a few seasons, was an experience. He was a great defender but he could be like a policeman on traffic duty in attempting to organise the defence. He would wave his arms about and tell us, 'You go there, you go to the other side and I'm staying right here because I'm the best header of the ball.'

I remember a game against Sheffield Wednesday when we were two goals up and he went down the middle of the field on an attacking run. Suddenly the move broke down and Wednesday broke away. A ball was played in and I jumped with one of their guys but he got above me and buried the ball in the back of our net. When Jack got back he gave me a right ear bashing. 'Every time I leave the middle, look what the hell happens. None of you can head a ball,' he bellowed. It didn't help soon afterwards when the Owls scored again to level it at 2–2. I made amends later and ended up the hero when I scored the winner with a free kick.

That wasn't my first goal for the club, which came against Middlesbrough at home on 6 October, just five games after I made my debut. I hit the ball from 25 yards out and the keeper should have saved it. He could really have thrown his cap on it and stopped it but, fortunately for me, he fluffed it. We lost the game 3–2. I scored once more in my first season, away at Charlton in April – a header from a corner. That was one in the eye for Syd Owen and Jack, who had both said I couldn't head a ball.

We finished the season in fifth place – a major improvement on 1961–62 when we had escaped relegation to the Third Division by the skin of our teeth. Revie was delighted and understandably so. The youngsters who were thrown in at the deep end at Swansea had repaid the faith he had shown in them and his signings had played their parts to the full, none more so than Jim Storrie. He had the goalscoring knack although the ball didn't always go in off his head or his boots. It would fly in off his knees, his thighs, almost any part of his body – but in it went, which was the main thing. He had the ability to be in the right places. During that 1962–63 season, Jim netted 25 goals in 38 league appearances. Albert Johanneson chipped in with 13 from 41 appearances at outside-left while Billy Bremner, playing at inside-right, scored 10 goals in 24 league games. Former Rotherham forward Don Weston totalled seven goals in 15 league outings and Bobby Collins hit eight goals in 41 league matches. In all we scored 79 goals in the league campaign, hardly the record of a dour side, as some had labelled us.

As for me, I was an ever-present in the side after making my debut at Swansea. I made 36 successive league appearances and played in our three FA Cup ties and in two League Cup ties. I never looked back.

4

TOP FLIGHT, MY BELOVED RED VIVA AND A £17 WAGE RISE

YOU COULD almost hear the laughter ringing throughout the whole of English football when Don Revie declared, 'We're going to become a Real Madrid. One day, we'll rule in Europe.' We were languishing in the Second Division and here was this young and untried manager making what could best be described as a rash statement.

He was ridiculed for it in the press and most of our fans thought he was mad, too – not to mention the players. When he told us, we all looked at one another and you could see most of the lads were thinking, 'Oh yes, and pigs might fly.' Not me, though. I took it as read. I totally and utterly believed in Don Revie.

Big in stature, he had great presence – one of those people who could walk up to a crowded bar and get served right away – and he was very determined in his single-minded quest for managerial success. You could not fail to be swept along on that wave of enthusiasm. Besides, if it had not been for him, I would not have realised my dream of becoming a professional footballer.

He had shown faith in me and I had total faith in him. As far as I was concerned, if he said it, it was right.

The club colours were even changed from dark blue shirts with gold collars, white shorts and blue and gold hooped socks to an all-white strip, emulating Real Madrid and still worn by the current Leeds team.

Revie's bold assertion faced us with a huge challenge. The first thing we had to do was hoist ourselves out of the Second Division. Having reached fifth place in the 1962–63 season, we were fancied to do well in the next campaign. Interest in the club had been rekindled with the average attendance going up from about 12,000 per game to something near 18,000. Appetites had been whetted and expectations were understandably higher than they had been for some time.

Before the start of the season the Gaffer called us all together and told us just how we were going to win promotion. We weren't likely to win the League Cup or the FA Cup and we desperately wanted to restore top-flight football to Elland Road, so it had to be our main objective. I was looking forward to my first full season in the senior team.

During the previous season, I'd discovered just how superstitious the Gaffer could be. On one occasion, just before we left the dressing room to go out for a match, I happened to pick up a football and throw it to the skipper, Bobby Collins, who caught it. It was a spur of the moment thing. We went out and won the game and I thought no more about it, but as we were about to leave the dressing room for the next match, the Gaffer came up to me and said, 'Norman, haven't you forgotten something?'

'I don't think so,' I replied.

'Yes, you have. Pick the football up and throw it to Bobby.'

From then on I had to go through that little ritual every time I played. A change of captain made no difference. Whoever had the role I still had to throw the ball to him. I don't know what would have happened if I had been captain, but he never made me captain – perhaps that was the reason why!

The Gaffer used to wear the same shirt, tie and suit all season if we made a good start and he felt it was a lucky outfit. In those days, mohair suits were popular but they tended to become very shiny and wear thin quite quickly. So by the time the end of the season was near, his suit would be looking the worse for wear. The story goes that at one Cup final we reached, Revie insisted on wearing the suit he had worn all season but on the big day the zip on his trousers broke. He resorted to using a safety pin rather than changing out of his lucky suit.

Although I have never been superstitious, I have to admit that I came to regard certain items as being lucky and continued to wear them longer than perhaps I might have done. I also used to get dressed in the same way for every game. I'd put my slips on first, then my socks, and I'd rub oil on my legs before pulling on my shorts and my boots. Last thing I'd do was put my shirt on.

We all got into the habit of doing things in certain ways. Everyone had a preferred place in line in the tunnel so we ran out in the same order every time. Jack Charlton liked to come out last. Eddie Gray pushed a photograph of his wife, Linda, down one of his socks when he played, although he didn't make it too obvious to us at the time. It was only later that we found out about it.

Later on, after we'd made it into the First Division and had been pipped at the post in the League and lost a Cup final, Revie arranged for a gypsy to visit to Elland Road. Apparently, he had been told that before the ground was used for football, gypsies had camped there and when they were ordered off to make way for the stadium, they had put a curse on the land. Don thought this was preventing us from taking the top prizes and asked the gypsy to come and lift the curse.

The players often talked about being superstitious but I don't believe the things we did made a scrap of difference to whether we won a game or not. Once you get into these habits, however, it's difficult to stop – and Revie would not hear of it. His way of doing things was the right way.

We kicked off the 1963–64 campaign with an unspectacular 1–0 home win over Rotherham United, our goal being scored by Don Weston. It was tremendously hard to win promotion from the Second Division, which was an extremely physical league. Wherever you went, it was always a big challenge. To have a chance, you had no alternative really but to be physical. We fought a long-running battle with Sunderland in particular, and Preston North End and Norwich City to a lesser degree, although we appeared to have a running feud with nearly everyone we played against. That's how it was. We thrived on our reputation and the Gaffer added to it. He used to instil into us that it was 'us' against 'them' and he never used to hide what people were saying or writing about us. As far as the rivalry with Sunderland was concerned, that was intensified when we were promoted together with Leeds as champions, and we stayed ahead of them until the 1973 FA Cup final.

One game that sticks in my mind from that promotion season was against Northampton Town. They had come up from the Third Division with a big reputation for being tough. They could 'put it about a bit' we were told and as we could also mix it with the best, the game was billed as a major battle. I think they were very near the top of the Second Division when we went down to their place to play them, quite early in the campaign. We were fully prepared for it, determined that they were not going to get the better of us, and the game lived up to all the pre-match hype. It was a humdinger. We might as well have left the ball in the dressing room for the first twenty-five minutes. Revie used to say to us that, first of all, we had to win the right to play and then, once that had been achieved, let our football do the talking – advice that still applies in the Premiership today. Gradually, we won the battle with Northampton and ran out 3–0 winners. Bobby Collins set the seal on a very satisfying victory by scoring the third goal. Ian Lawson and Don Weston got the others. We were good at winning the physical battles – we had the right players and the desire to win.

As it transpired, the Gaffer had been working behind the scenes before the season started to make a signing – Johnny Giles from Manchester United. He'd hit the jackpot when he signed Bobby Collins from Everton and he hit it again with Johnny.

A right-winger at that time, Johnny was twenty-two years old when he left Old Trafford in August 1963 in what was reported to be a £33,000 transfer. In those days, it was relatively straight-forward to sign a player. You didn't have two or three agents complicating the issue. If a club wanted to sell and the player was willing to move, you made the arrangements and got on with the deal. These days, agents play a huge role in transfers, especially the mega-money moves, and if you believe the stories you read in the newspapers, they can make an astronomical amount of money. They can also cause problems by touting players around and leaking stories to the press. I suppose that, as in any walk of life, there are good ones and bad ones and I do think that, with the amount of money a good young player can earn, with the opportunity for merchandising, advertising and sponsorship, a good agent is essential. Frankly, though, I wouldn't like to have to deal with them and I shudder to think what Don Revie and Bill Shankly would have made of agents. They just wouldn't have tolerated them. In their day, players who had a chance to play for Liverpool or Leeds United jumped at it because they were big and successful clubs. When I was a young player, we didn't have advisers and I didn't really feel the need to drive a hard bargain over money because I was just delighted to be playing professional football. Maybe we were exploited to an extent. We certainly weren't in with a chance of becoming millionaires as a lot of today's star players are. But just as mobile phones have become a part of everyday life now, agents are part of football and I think there is a need for stricter control because of the money they take out of the game.

It didn't take all that long for Leeds and Manchester United to agree Johnny's move and he came straight into the side for the second game of the season, another home clash, this time against Bury, which we won 3–0. We drew at Rotherham in our third outing. Not quite Real Madrid stuff just yet but at least the Whites were on their way.

Although we lost 3–2 at Manchester City in the next game, that proved to be a blip because we then built a great unbeaten run of twenty games winning twelve and drawing the other eight. We beat Portsmouth, Norwich City, Northampton Town, Scunthorpe United, Middlesbrough, Huddersfield Town, Southampton, Grimsby Town, Leyton Orient, Swansea Town, Plymouth Argyle and Bury, drawing with Swindon Town, Portsmouth, Cardiff City, Derby County, Charlton Athletic, Preston North End, Northampton and Sunderland. That sequence set us up as serious promotion contenders. Our aim was always to adopt an 'up and at 'em' policy and we hardly ever began a game in a slow tempo. We were always psyched up for matches and that suited me fine because I was on a knife-edge before going out. The Gaffer never attempted to calm me down. It suited us and stood us in good stead.

The last game in that unbeaten run was a 1–1 draw against our chief rivals, Sunderland, at Elland Road on Boxing Day. Sunderland got their revenge two days later when they beat us 2–0 at Roker Park. They were a good side. Jim Montgomery was their keeper. Jim was to have arguably the greatest moment of his career when he denied us a goal with a brilliant save in the 1973 FA Cup final at Wembley. Charlie Hurley and Len Ashurst were in defence and Nicky Sharkey, George Herd, Johnny Crossan and George Mulhall were among their attacking players, so they were no mugs.

The points they took from us in those two games piled on the pressure. We certainly were not having things all our own way and we needed a boost. The Gaffer knew it and he provided it shortly after that defeat at Roker Park by making another signing. With Jim Storrie out of the side through injury we had begun to run short on goals and in a bid to remedy that problem Alan Peacock was brought in. Alan was an England international and had played alongside Brian Clough at Middlesbrough. He had netted 126 goals in 218 appearances for them, but Revie had taken something of a gamble again because he had had knee problems. However, he turned up trumps for us, playing in our last fourteen league games, scoring eight goals and putting the finishing touches to our season.

Alan led the front line so well and was a great header of the ball. Despite having dodgy knees he was still a very fit man. In the gym the weights he could lift were amazing. I could hardly move them while he lifted them with ease. I remembered having played against him and thinking what a good player he was, so I was delighted when we bought him.

We made sure of promotion with two matches remaining after we won 3–0 at Swansea in a game that marked the first-team debut of Terry Cooper. But we wanted the title and with Sunderland still breathing down our necks we knew we could not afford to lose our nerve. Having clinched promotion, we did a lap of honour before our penultimate game of the season, at home to Plymouth Argyle, who were fighting against relegation, but we slipped up and had to settle for a 1–1 draw. Sunderland picked up maximum points from a 2–1 win at home to Charlton and closed the gap between us to just one point. So it all hinged on the final day of the season when we had to travel to Charlton while Sunderland visited Grimsby Town. I'm happy to report we won the day. Peacock scored twice as we beat Charlton 2–0 and Sunderland were held to a 2–2 draw to leave us title winners with a two-point margin. Our points tally of 63 was the highest any Second Division side had amassed since Tottenham totalled 70 in 1920.

We had again leaned heavily on Bobby Collins, especially when the going got tough, learning from his great experience and football knowledge. He led by example and was the rock on which we built our success. Bobby missed just one of our 42 league games and netted six goals.

I played in every one of our games and managed to score a couple of goals – one at home to Middlesbrough in a 2–0 win and the other in a 2–2 draw at Swindon.

We had a great finish to the season, winning eight and drawing two of our final ten games to go up as champions, but most people thought that Sunderland were the better side and that we would be back down again at the end of our first season in the top flight.

We weren't rated very highly. People seemed to think that we were just a hard, grafting side. That acted as a spur to us. We never went into games thinking we would lose. Whether that was down to Don Revie or the players, I don't know, but we were supremely confident. Even when we made a good start and found ourselves near the top of the First Division I never once thought, 'What are we doing here?' I always thought we belonged in the top flight. It was natural to play top sides and win.

In our promotion season we hadn't lost a single home league game and Elland Road was beginning to seem something of a fortress. We were a force to be reckoned with there and teams worried about coming to our ground, which was just what we wanted. Away from home we weren't that bad either. We lost just three times during our promotion campaign – at Sunderland, Manchester City and Preston. I think that was a record for a promotion-winning side. We ended up with 24 victories and 15 draws from our 42 league games and were very proud of those results.

The film-star lives of today's top players contrast sharply with the lifestyles of top English footballers of the 1960s and 1970s. When Leeds United won promotion my wage was £13 a week plus £5 appearance money, so during the summer months it was just the £13 a week. After reaching the First Division, Revie put us up to £35 a week with no appearance money and for that we had to sign for the club for a few years. He wanted to cut it down during the close season but we banded together and resisted that.

A system of bonuses pushed the money up a bit. We got a crowd bonus, for instance, that paid extra if attendances went above a certain figure – 35,000, I think it was – and eventually win bonuses were brought in. I remember my wife, Susie, commenting, 'Heavens, if we don't win, Norm, we're in trouble.' You know what it's like when you get married, buy a house and take on a mortgage, and I had also bought a small house in Leeds for my mother. The biggest bonus we were ever on at Leeds was £2,000 to win the League or the FA Cup. It was never £4,000 or £5,000 because the Gaffer knew that somewhere along the line we were likely to be involved in at least one of the competitions and if he had put us on £5,000, the club would have had to pay out a lot more money.

We weren't paupers by any means and compared to the man in the street we were better paid. However, I can honestly say that money was never the real motivation for me. Playing football was what mattered. Looking back, maybe money should have been more of a motivation because it's a short career and when you finish playing you need to have something to soften the blow, but I was happy enough and the last thing in the world I thought about was leaving Leeds United. I loved the club and loved playing for it. We all had tremendous loyalty to Leeds United but, in any case, you never got to know if other clubs were interested in you or if there had been any offers for

ung hopefuls – I'm on the left, with fellow sixteen-year-old groundstaff boys, Rod Johnson *ntre*) and Stuart Silverwood.

st taste of success – Leeds United's Second Division title-winning side of 1963–64 with championship trophy *(centre)* and the West Riding Senior Cup. *Left to right (back row):* lie Bell, Paul Reaney, Freddie Goodwin, Gary Sprake, Brian Williamson, me, Ian Lawson. *ont row):* Johnny Giles, Billy Bremner, Jim Storrie, Bobby Collins, Don Revie, Don Weston, my Greenhoff, Jack Charlton.

The Gentle Giant, John Charles, in action against Stoke City in August 1962 during his first game for Leeds United following his return from Juventus. Bobby Collins looks on.

Watching brief – I'm casting an anxious lo as Jack Charlton and Gary Sprake deal wit a goal attempt during the 1965 FA Cup fi against Liverpool.

There's no way through for Liverpool on this occasion as the famed Leeds defence goes into action. Billy Bremner (No. 4) and Paul Reaney guard the goalline while Bobby Collins prods the ball back to Gary Sprake with Jack Charlton (grounded) having tackled Roger Hunt. Johnny Giles and I look on.

on men – I was determined to beat my old mate and Liverpool foe Tommy Smith to the ball…

…and I did, though he slid in for the tackle.

Early days in Europe – emerging from the underground dressing rooms at Dinamo Zagreb for the first leg of the 1967 Inter Cities Fairs Cup final. Billy Bremner leads the way ahead of Gary Sprake and Eddie Gray, followed by me. Behind is Mike O'Grady. We lost 2–0 and then drew 0–0 at Elland Road.

Watching the action are Don Revie, who played such a great part in my career, and trainer Les Cocker, who toughened me up.

Syd Owen, another member of the Revie backroom team to whom I owe so much, shows a group of apprentices how it should be done.

er a few near misses we win our first
phy, the 1968 League Cup, and Don
ie and Les Cocker show their
ght.

Jack Charlton and Gary Sprake hoist skipper Billy
Bremner aloft as he shows off the League Cup. I'm
on the right and on the left are Johnny Giles (*front*)
Eddie Gray and Paul Reaney.

's presence on the goalline always made life difficult for goalkeepers. Here he challenges
nal's Jim Furnell but it was Paul Madeley (hidden) who challenged the keeper more
ngly on this occasion and when the ball went out to Terry Cooper, he hammered it into the
for the only goal of the final.

With my mum, Betty, in 1968, looking at the scrapbook she kept of my career.

With Sue on our wedding day, 11 June 1968.

Another picture for the wedding album. *From left to right*: Linda and Eddie Gray, Sue and m and Kathy and Gary Sprake.

ight: In the garden with
n Michael (three) and
ughter Claire (eighteen
onths).

low: At home with the
mily.

Mick Jones displays courage and determination to score the only goal of the 1968 Fairs Cup final first leg at Elland Road against Ferencvaros.

The goal was enough to earn us our second trophy as we drew the return leg in Hungary 0–0 thanks to a fine defensive display. Here I'm clearing the ball from Florian Albert.

you. It was only much later on when players were getting older and leaving the club that the Gaffer told us there had been offers virtually every week for one or other of us in the earlier days. He also told us that whenever he used to approach clubs for players they would say, 'OK, you can have so and so but give me Bremner or Hunter or Giles.'

There was no such thing as a club car in those days so we had to buy our own. We got £1,000 for winning the Second Division championship and after tax I was left with about £600. I bought a red Vauxhall Viva with it and it was my pride and joy. I'd had it about a week when I drove to meet Alan Peacock and Jimmy Greenhoff at Middleton Golf Club in Leeds. There wasn't another car in the car park as I proudly parked my car alongside Alan's. Suddenly Jimmy Greenhoff came roaring in, slammed on his brakes and skidded right into the back of my beloved Viva.

The only time I had a car provided for me was when I made the England World Cup squad in 1966 and we were all provided with a Ford Cortina GT. It was a lovely car – white with the registration GWC, standing for Great World Cup. As I was usually a substitute, because of Bobby Moore's presence, the number on my car was 12. They were great number plates and we should all have kept them, but we didn't. We were allowed to use the cars for twelve months after which we were able to purchase them at a knock-down price.

My best salary was £12,500 a year, which I earned when I was thirty-five and playing for Bristol City. Some of the players were on more than that. Having been with Leeds for all those years and played at the top of my profession, I found it astonishing that I could earn more at Bristol City. We had all been wrapped up in playing for Leeds United and never really got top money. We were certainly the poor relations when it came to comparing our wages with those at some of the London clubs.

After four seasons in the Second Division, it gave us great pleasure to prove all the dismal Johnnies wrong. Not only did we not go straight back down again, we finished runners-up to Manchester United for the First Division championship on goal average, reached the final of the FA Cup and qualified for Europe. That was one in the eye for the knockers who said we were just a bunch of cloggers with no class and no skills, young upstarts from the north who would soon be put in our place. We were aggressive all right and we might have bent the rules a bit here and there but we certainly had skill in the side, which developed over time.

Revie had got together a group of players whom he welded into a unit, the unit got better and the players within that unit got better. We had a game plan – and the famous dossiers he compiled on the opposition. We marked areas of the pitch rather than players. Contrary to what many people seemed to believe, it was not Revie's plan to play defensively. I can't recall him instructing us to get everyone behind the ball but we always seemed to end up in a defensive situation whenever we went a goal up in an away game. It just happened and got to the stage where people would say, 'Oh, that's it, they've won it.' More often than not they were right because we did have a great defence and we knew our business. If we had carried on playing as we were before going ahead, we may well have won games more comfortably but we usually put in a hard defensive performance. Eventually, we established ourselves as a good side and then we used to run all over the opposition. In fact, if we hadn't gone three goals up in the first twenty minutes of a home game, the crowd would begin to moan!

5

BITING BACK
AT BIG JACK
AND CONFOUNDING
THE CRITICS

SUCCESS doesn't always bring acceptance, as we soon found out. 'The team people love to hate' was the label the press gave us. Outside our own supporters, nobody liked us. We were dour, physical, over-aggressive – you name it and it was said or written about us. Don Revie would bring in the cuttings to show us, in case we hadn't seen them already. 'Look what they're writing about us now,' he'd say. 'We'll show 'em.' He used the criticism to help make us into a team who would do anything for each other so that if someone touched one of us, he touched us all. The Gaffer was brilliant. Nothing went amiss. His attention to detail was amazing but what made him such a great manager was that he could always get the very best out of his players.

For me, life was good – marvellous in fact. There I was, playing football and getting paid for it and we were about to lock horns with the best teams in England, having earned the right to do so. Each morning when I woke up I could not wait to get out on the training pitch, just across the car park from the stadium, because training was so enjoyable. We were all facing up to a massive challenge and relishing it. The Gaffer knew when to put an arm round you and give you a bit of encouragement but he knew, too, how to give you a kick up the backside, though not literally. He was a little more subtle than that.

When we experienced a bad time, which thankfully was not very often, he used to threaten us with the chequebook. That really annoyed us. He would walk into the dressing room waving a chequebook about and tell us he would use it to buy new players if we didn't improve. I well remember the time – 1973–74 it was – he used that ploy after a twenty-nine game unbeaten run. We lost 3–2 at Stoke and in he walked with the chequebook held aloft, threatening to replace us. Can you imagine that!

In August 1964, however, all we had on our minds was getting to grips with top-flight football. Hopes were high and the future looked bright. The players were buzzing, as were the fans, and Elland Road was just a great place to be. Come Saturday, none of us could wait to get out on the pitch and play. We got off to a flying start by winning 2–1 at Aston Villa and I have to confess that I cannot really remember much about it. But I can certainly remember our first home game. It was against Liverpool. They arrived as the reigning First Division champions and, as we had been promoted after finishing top of the Second, the meeting was billed as a battle of the champions – and what a game it turned out to be. Over 36,000 fans came to watch and we won 4–2. Ron Yeats was playing in defence for them and their goalkeeper was Tommy Lawrence. Gordon Milne, Peter Thompson, Roger Hunt and Ian Callaghan, who all became internationals, were in the side that day as was Ronnie Moran, who later became a member of the famous Anfield bootroom. They were at the beginning of what was to prove a great era for Liverpool and all those players became household names.

I remember our performance that day as being very much a team effort. Everyone put in the extra effort but we also played some neat and creative football. We went ahead after about quarter of an hour when Albert Johanneson's shot was diverted in off Yeats' shoulder and although Liverpool pulled level through Hunt, we went on to open up a 4–1 lead with goals from Don Weston, Billy Bremner and Johnny Giles. The crowd could hardly believe it and neither could we but the chant went up 'We want five' – and this against the reigning champions. We couldn't oblige and while Liverpool hit back with a second goal, from Milne, we deserved to be the glory boys on this occasion. We never allowed ourselves to feel inferior to anybody for the simple reason that we didn't think we were. No one had done us any favours. We were there because we were good enough.

We beat Wolves at home in the next game, making it three straight wins, and we'd scored nine goals – not a bad start for so-called cloggers and no-hopers. For our fourth game – the return with Liverpool – nearly 53,000 fans filled Anfield, which was the biggest crowd we had played in front of at that time. But it wasn't so much the size of the crowd that impressed me, more the atmosphere the fans created. I thought it was a fantastic place – and still do. When the Kop sang 'You'll Never Walk Alone' the hairs on the back of my neck stood up. Even now, when I go back to Anfield in my role as a radio summariser, it sends a shiver down my spine when they sing that song. I would say it was my favourite ground after Elland Road. There's something about Anfield that has to appeal to you and I always found their supporters very knowledgeable about the game and fair-minded.

Liverpool gained their revenge on us with a 2–1 win and I think that was the start of the tremendous respect that developed between the clubs. There was never any animosity between the clubs or the players. We always had very hard games against them but there was never any bad blood between us. When I was first selected in a full England squad, I knocked about with the Liverpool lads. Apart from Jack Charlton, I was the only Leeds player there. Bill Shankly and Don Revie had a healthy respect for each other, too, and talked on the telephone every Sunday to discuss what had gone on the day before.

Our intense rivalry with Sunderland carried on in the fifth game of the season, at Roker Park, and a right old battle it turned out to be. Jim Storrie, Willie Bell and Albert Johanneson scored our goals in a 3–3 draw and Brian Clough, who some years later was the controversial choice as successor to Don Revie at Leeds, opened the scoring for the home side. The ball passed over my head and he came in behind me and headed it in at the far post. He was just back in the side following a spell out with a knee injury and I think that was the last goal of his playing career. He never really recovered from the injury. Northern Ireland international Johnny Crossan scored the other two. We had actually gone two goals up but Sunderland hit back to take a 3–2 lead before I set up a chance for Albert who notched the equaliser.

With our unbeaten run intact we set off for the seaside for our next game but came down to earth with a bang as Blackpool walloped us 4–0. A little lad by the name of Alan Ball was playing for them and Don Revie had given me the job of marking him tightly to keep him out of the game. I gave him some stick and kept on tackling him but he kept bouncing up like a Jack-in-the-Box and getting back on the ball. I marked him man-to-man – or rather I tried to – but he absolutely destroyed me that day. That experience didn't dent my confidence and in the return game, which wasn't long in coming, revenge was sweet. Having beaten Leicester City at Elland Road, Blackpool were our visitors and we beat them 3–0. Bobby Collins scored twice and I got the other. Jimmy Armfield, later manager of Leeds, claims that we kicked lumps out of them in the second game. That might well have been the case – I can't remember – but we won and that was the main thing. There was no denying that Alan Ball was a very good player. Revie came to admire him greatly and was very keen to sign him for Leeds. I think we were actually on the point of getting him until Everton came in at the last minute and snatched him away from us.

The one big disappointment of that season came towards the end when Manchester United visited Elland Road. Conditions were far from ideal. It was windy, the pitch was rock hard and bumpy and, as I recall, it had been covered by tons of straw in a bid to keep it from freezing. Like us, they were making a bold bid to win the championship and they won the game 1–0 with a goal from John Connelly. I ran out to challenge him and attempted to block the ball but it dropped between him and Denis Law and Connelly turned and hit it. It wasn't really a good shot but because it went through my legs and there were a few other people about, Gary Sprake didn't have a good view of it. In fact, he didn't have a chance.

It was an atrocious game but it turned out to be a crucial victory for Manchester United because they pipped us on goal average to take the title. If we had won that game, we could have gone on to clinch the championship. As we'd got nearer the end of the season, we'd realised we were in with a chance. We knew we could grind things out and were hard to beat, and we also had players who could score goals. However, with just one day to rest after the Manchester United game we had to play Sheffield Wednesday home and away on successive days. Having to play three games in four days was normal then. Somehow I don't think managers now would take too kindly to having a similar run of games.

The first meeting was at Hillsborough and we lost 3–0. The local newspaper said that we had gone stale and the Gaffer actually agreed with that. The season was taking its toll on us. It certainly was on me. I'm not blaming it entirely on fatigue but in that game I suffered the embarrassment of scoring an own goal – my first in senior football. Johnny Fantham scored their first two goals and mine was their third – a result of not being careful enough when passing the ball back. That defeat lost us the leadership of the First Division.

Twenty-four hours later Sheffield Wednesday came to Elland Road and we beat them 2–0. Jim Storrie put us ahead, Johnny Giles sealed the win with a well-taken penalty and back we went to the top. The game was notable for launching the career of Peter Lorimer. He didn't play in either of our remaining two fixtures but the Gaffer made him a regular the following season.

Next up was a trip to Bramall Lane, home of Wednesday's arch rivals Sheffield United. Mick Jones, who a few seasons later was to join Leeds United in a £100,000 transfer, played for the Blades but he was goalless on this occasion as we kept a clean sheet and put three past their defence, courtesy of Jim Storrie, Billy Bremner and Alan Peacock. That left us facing Birmingham City at St Andrews in our final game of the season. Birmingham were bottom of the table and already relegated while we were top when we went there. Although the Blues had to play with ten men for all but the first ten minutes of the game after right-winger Alex Jackson was taken off injured, they opened up a shock 3–0 lead. We hit back with a penalty from Johnny Giles. Then Paul Reaney marked the occasion by scoring the first league goal of his career before Jack Charlton knocked in the equaliser two minutes from the end. A point from the game wasn't enough and Manchester United, who also finished the season with 61 points, took the title because they had a better goal average.

While we had been making a strong push for the title, we had also fashioned a great run in the FA Cup, starting in January with a third-round victory against Southport. We needed a replay at Goodison Park to beat Everton in the fourth round and followed that with victories against Shrewsbury Town and Crystal Palace to reach a semi-final tie against Manchester United. After a goalless draw at Hillsborough we travelled to the City Ground in Nottingham for the replay where a back-header by Billy Bremner saw us through. The wee fella had a habit of coming up trumps at vital times and with that goal he booked us a trip to Wembley to play Liverpool in the final.

As a kid I'd dreamed about playing at Wembley, just like my boyhood hero Jackie Milburn had done all those years before me. It was every boy's ambition to play there. I hardly slept a wink the night before, tossing and turning in my bed, and I was up early, wandering around aimlessly. I wanted the kick-off to come quickly but I didn't want to get to the stadium too early. I hated arriving at 1.30 and having to hang around for an hour and a half. When we finally left our hotel on the outskirts of London I felt better. Travelling down Wembley Way on the team coach was a fantastic experience – one that I'll never forget. We were a young team and, of course, we hadn't experienced anything quite like that before. There were plenty of Liverpool fans there but I only really noticed the Leeds fans. They had turned out in their thousands to welcome us and it was an exciting and moving experience to see so many of them there. But once we got into the stadium it was a big let down. I was very disappointed, especially with the dressing rooms. I was expecting them to be something really special but they weren't. They were very old – and so was the stadium.

However, going out to look at the pitch was a great experience. Not many people were there then but running out later, ready to play in the Cup final, was something very special. I had to pinch myself to confirm that it really was happening to me and the sad thing is that the game had gone before I realised it.

As I've said, the season had taken a lot out of us and we could not have faced a harder team in the Cup final than Liverpool. They were just emerging as a major force in the game and were a couple of seasons ahead of us in their development. Although the final went to extra time and they eventually triumphed 2–1, the fact is they hammered us. Gary Sprake was absolutely outstanding, keeping us in the game with a string of fine saves when otherwise we might have been dead and buried. We'd just kicked off in extra time when Roger Hunt broke the stalemate with a headed goal. We pulled level a few minutes later. For some reason, Jack Charlton had stayed up after a corner. I knocked the ball to him, he jumped and headed it down and Billy Bremner hit it on the half volley. In it went and we were all ecstatic. It was a great goal. For five or ten minutes after that Liverpool were deflated. They had battered us and before that goal we just hadn't been at the races. Then all of a sudden we're back in it at 1–1. If we'd had a little more experience, perhaps we could have gone on to win it. We went at them for a bit but Ian St John settled it with a header.

The disappointment at losing the Cup final was bigger than missing out on the League. Confident though we were as a team, we didn't really feel at the start of the season that we would win the title. We did exceptionally well to push Manchester United all the way for the championship. The Cup final was a one-off situation. We felt we had a chance of winning it and when we didn't it was a massive blow. Liverpool were too good for us on the day and, dejected as we were, we had to accept that. All the same, our first season in the top flight was a fabulous experience for us. We had exceeded all expectations.

Don Revie was delighted. 'Go off and enjoy your holidays and I'll see you back for pre-season,' he told us. On orders from the Gaffer I always took my spikes with me when the close season began. 'Take them and try to get a bit quicker,' he would say.

As soon as pre-season training came round he would be in optimistic mood and tell us that we were going to win this, that or the other. Although I enjoyed the day-to-day training during the season, I hated doing the pre-season work. For me, it was the only downside to being a professional footballer. Pre-season work was just one hard slog. We would train at Temple Newsam, a large park on the outskirts of Leeds, and also at Roundhay Park where we used the infamous Hill Sixty, which we had to run up and down. We did that in the morning and again in the afternoon and it was very demanding physically. I could run all day up to a point but I was completely shattered at the end of a day of pre-season work. For the first week or ten days our pre-season schedule was running and more running. Then the Gaffer would introduce the ball. People used to remark to me how well organised as a team we were and say that we must have practised everything down to the last detail. Not so.

Once the season got under way we were physically very well prepared and training consisted mainly of five-a-side games. That's all we ever did apart from set-piece moves. Mind you, they were brilliant games. We played some of the best football you could ever wish to see in those five-a-side matches and they were always very keenly contested. We were all desperate to avoid having the infamous yellow jersey handed to us. The Gaffer introduced the yellow jersey soon after he became manager. We had to vote for the worst player in the five-a-side game and the unlucky one had to wear the jersey until we voted on it again. It had a big wooden spoon stitched across the front of it. If you got the yellow jersey you went home feeling very upset. I know I certainly did. I really felt offended and took it to heart. Thankfully, it didn't happen to me very often. Everybody would have a laugh at your expense and the Gaffer would tell you to take it in your stride and smile about it but that wasn't easy. We used to wind up Jack Charlton if we were struggling to find the worst player to vote for. We'd gang up on him and give him the vote just for a laugh. I'm not so sure he saw the funny side of it but, in any case, he just refused to wear it!

Jack was a bit of a law unto himself. I never actually heard him refer to Revie as Gaffer or Boss or use either of those terms when he spoke to him. He just didn't call him anything. If he ever talks about him these days, he refers to him as Revie. I don't really know why but maybe it was because they had played at the same time. Of course, Jack was older than the rest of us and about eight years younger than the Gaffer so maybe that had something to do with it. I do think Jack had an awful lot of respect for the Gaffer. He owed him a lot because Jack was going nowhere in the game until Revie came.

Jack was a bit unruly and would lose his temper in the dressing room. Jack tells a tale that Revie once informed him that if he could manage to stop messing about, take his job more seriously and concentrate on doing what he was good at, he would play for England. Jack said that when he heard that he laughed out loud, but what happened not too long afterwards? Jack was selected for England. Revie was a good judge of a player and Jack, who had maybe not realised just how much he had going for him, heeded the advice. He had to buckle down under Revie or he would have been out on his ear.

Jack was a late developer – he was nearly thirty when he won his first England cap – but he was never short on confidence and was always quick to give vent to his feelings and let you know what he thought of you or your mistakes. Alan Humphreys was one of our goalkeepers in the early 1960s. He didn't make all that many first-team appearances but I never saw a player get told off as much by a centre-half as Alan did. Jack was always on at him.

I can recall an incident in a game against West Ham when I was trying to mark Clyde Best, a massive man. Clyde got above me to a crossed ball and headed against the bar. That didn't go down at all well with Jack. He mouthed off at me and I totally lost my temper, screaming at him in return. Our fans in the old 'Scratching Shed' at Elland Road were encouraging me, shouting, 'Go on, Norm, tell him what you think.' I felt good at the time but when we came off at the end I thought I would be in for a right going over from the big man and I decided to get in first.

'Jack, I'm very sorry,' I said.

'Ah, don't worry, Norm. It's over and done with and forgotten,' he replied.

You could have a stand-up shouting match with him but Jack never held a grudge. It was the first time I had had a go back at him but I felt I had a case. Clyde Best stood about 6ft 3ins tall and it should have been Jack who was marking him.

I'll tell you something about Jack – he was great to play with. With his big loping strides he may not have looked it but he was quick. We used to like it when someone got him annoyed. If someone managed that there was not a better centre-half in the game than Jack. He was a very good player – a great player in many ways once he had buckled down to the job in hand. I have never known any player who, from a standing jump, could get as high as Jack. His nickname was 'The Giraffe'. He had a long neck and a phenomenal spring and he was a great header of the ball. He was also a very brave player. I remember him playing with a broken nose for six weeks and he went up for headers – and won them – without even flinching.

What Jack got out of the game he fully deserved because he earned it. In a five-year association with England he made 35 full appearances and, of course, picked up a World Cup winners' medal after England's 4–2 triumph over West Germany in the 1966 final at Wembley. He also proved to be a great servant for Leeds United. He was at the club for 21 years, made 772 first-team appearances and scored 94 goals. You won't get many – if indeed any – modern-day players showing that kind of loyalty to one club and amassing that sort of record. Moving around was not as easy in those days, of course, and quite a lot of us who were involved in the successful years of the Revie era made hundreds of first-team appearances for the club. Billy Bremner played in 770 games and hit the target 115 times while Paul Reaney appeared 734 times with nine goals to his name I made 722 appearances for the club and netted 21 goals.

Back in 1965, though, none of us thought about totting up so many games for the club. It had been a good season for the club and international recognition was now on the agenda for some of us. Jack picked up his first England cap against Scotland in 1965 but I had actually been involved with the full international squad in October 1964, when England were due to play Belgium. I was taken along mainly to get a taste of what preparations were like at national level. I don't think there was ever any chance of me playing in that game. I played in a Football League side against the Irish League on 28 October 1964 in Belfast, a game we won 4–0, and then made my debut for the England Under-23s against Wales at Wrexham on 4 November 1964.

Playing for the Under-23 side was a step up the career ladder for me. Martin Chivers, Alan Ball, John Sissons, Len Badger and Cyril Knowles were some of the other players in the team and I found it a great experience. It proved to be quite an open game but we ran out 3–2 winners. I can't recall who the goalscorers were but I wasn't among them.

At the end of the 1964–65 season Paul Reaney and I were included in the England Under-23 squad to play matches in Germany, Czechoslovakia and Austria. I had also been named as reserve for the full England side to play against Hungary at Wembley. Unfortunately for me, a knee injury I picked up in the FA Cup final against Liverpool forced me to withdraw from both squads and I had to wait a little longer for my full England debut. It was a disappointment but at the age of twenty-one time was on my side.

We had made club history by taking Leeds United into European competition for the first time. Bobby Collins had been a tower of strength and was rewarded for his efforts by being voted Footballer of the Year by the Football Writers' Association. He also earned a recall to the Scotland side at the age of thirty-four, after an absence of six years. Yes, 1964–65 had been a notable season.

6

MIDFIELD MARVELS, EUROPEAN BAPTISM AND CARPET BOWLS

THERE was a definite buzz in the air as we reported back to prepare for the 1965–66 season, which was only to be expected. I couldn't wait to get started again. We had done ourselves proud in our first season in top-flight football and we now had the added incentive of taking part in the Inter Cities Fairs Cup – the European competition that preceded the UEFA Cup.

We made a fine start to the First Division programme, losing only two games out of the first ten leading up to our debut in Europe against Italian side Torino. This was a game we were really looking forward to and we were determined to enjoy ourselves. The atmosphere was terrific. Billy Bremner scored our first goal and Alan Peacock the second just before half-time but Torino hit back with a goal ten minutes from the end, leaving us with a 2–1 first-leg lead. We should have had more goals because we created a lot of chances but their goalkeeper, Vieri, pulled off some fine saves. Torino returned to Italy feeling they had a good chance in the second leg at their place but we turned in a great display to earn a goalless draw.

However, our joy at reaching the second round was marred by a serious injury to Bobby Collins. I can still remember the tackle that put him out of the game and left us to battle for forty minutes with only ten men. Bobby and I were both well up the field when I saw a big defender coming towards him. Bobby was extremely quick over five to ten yards and he knocked the ball forward and accelerated after it but the big guy didn't pull up. He kept on running and his knee went right into Bobby's thigh. When I got to Bobby, his leg was waving around at the top because the bone was snapped high up the leg. It was horrendous. I don't think that sort of injury had ever been heard of in a football game before. They mostly happened in car accidents. It was a massive blow for Bobby personally because it's hard to come back from serious injury at thirty-five years of age. It was also a great blow to the club because he meant so much to the team. He was the rock around which it had been built. Bobby was out of the game for almost twelve months and made just a few more appearances for us before moving to Burnley. He surprised everyone by coming back at all.

More immediately, we were faced with the problem of replacing an experienced, talented and gutsy midfield player upon whom we had come to rely heavily. We hadn't reckoned on Johnny Giles. Johnny was signed purely as a winger. He joined Manchester United as a midfield player but they played him on the wing and so did Don Revie. But once Johnny took over in midfield for us he was absolutely fantastic. He formed a partnership with Billy Bremner that can only be described as magnificent. They were naturals. Bobby had set the way we played and instilled the high level of commitment and the will to win, but Gilesy took playing in midfield to another level.

In many ways Giles and Bremner were opposites. Johnny would drop back deep to gain possession and ping the ball here, there and everywhere with great accuracy whereas Billy could do things with the ball I could only dream about. He would do the unexpected and score spectacular goals. Johnny was the one that few people in the crowd really noticed whereas Billy, being a fiery character, almost always took the eye. Billy was an inspirational player who would have you on the edge of your seat. He was exciting to watch whereas Johnny controlled midfield in a less energetic way. The combination was extremely efficient and productive. Both were able to dictate a game. Johnny and Bobby Collins were the best I've seen at being able to get hold of a game by the scruff of the neck and direct it.

Gilesy was a dedicated trainer but Billy was probably one of the worst trainers you could ever come across, especially with cross-country running or anything like that. He hated training unless a ball was involved. Then he would run all day. He was brilliant in five-a-side games but on the rare occasions we trained without a ball he really didn't want to know. Yet he was a very fit person.

The pair of them had the ability and know-how to change things on the field. If the game wasn't going right for us, they would instinctively change tactics without any instructions from the bench. If someone in the opposition was having a great game, the shout would go up, 'Hey, get a grip of him,' and make no mistake about it we would. I sit and watch football now and wonder sometimes what players are thinking about. I was a defender and when I got that ball I was not supposed to lose possession. If I gave it away, Gilesy or Billy would give me the biggest rollocking. I couldn't really win, though, because if I passed to Billy, I would get a mouthful from Gilesy, and if I gave it to Gilesy I would get a rebuke from Billy. That's how keen they were to be involved and it was a joy to play with them. How Johnny found space I don't know but he would be there. 'Yes, Norm,' he would shout and if he happened to be marked, you could bet your bottom dollar that Billy would be there waiting for the pass.

I know that teams used to set out with the intention of stopping Giles and Bremner, the theory being that if they were successful, Leeds would struggle, but that wasn't the case at all. I would have hated to play against them and it was almost impossible to blot both of them out of a game but if it happened, there were other options. To my right I had Peter Lorimer and Paul Reaney and sometimes Paul Madeley, while to my left there was Terry Cooper and Eddie Gray. On the rare occasions I found it necessary to whack the ball upfield, Allan Clarke and Mick Jones were there. Terrible options for anyone weren't they? It was very hard to stop the Leeds team of our era because, as with all great teams, there was always someone available for you to pass the ball to – and I knew that if I took up a good position upfield, I would get the ball passed to me. Manchester United do it these days. If players go forward from the back, they will invariably get the ball given to them. It is a sign of a good and talented side. I used to go on overlaps, too, but that didn't go down at all well with Jack Charlton. When I got back he'd shout, 'Where the hell have you been?'

We were a good side with some tremendous players and, contrary to what many people used to think and what was often written about us, Revie did not put us under strict instructions to stay back and not go forward. Initially, he used to stress to me that my job was to win the ball and knock it to those who could play, which used to annoy me because I thought I could play a bit but the Gaffer wouldn't have it. 'Norman,' he'd say, 'you win it and if Johnny is there give the ball to him or if Billy is there give it to him.' At first I used to carry out my instructions to the letter but once I was settled in and was playing well I would think nothing of going forward and joining the attack. I was totally confident and went through a spell where I tried to nutmeg opponents. It's always a crowd pleaser if you beat someone by knocking it through his legs. I got away with it once or twice but in one game against Leicester City I tried to nutmeg Frank Worthington. This time it didn't come off. Frank took the ball off me and chipped it towards goal. Fortunately for me, it went just wide. As you might imagine, the big man gave me a real going over. I knew I was in for it as soon as I lost possession. 'Serves you right,' he bellowed. 'Don't you dare do that again. You just win the bloody thing and give it to Eddie, Johnny or Billy.' Not wishing to bear the brunt of Jack's tongue again, for the next few weeks whenever I got the ball I just hit it upfield.

But when you play with such great players, you have to try a few things yourself. That's the way I looked at it anyway, even though I got some right rollockings. If it wasn't Jack it would be Gilesy or Billy. If I felt I was having a good game and things were going our way, I might try a few things and be pleased to get away with them, but Gilesy would say, 'I know you did all right but you wait until you're on a bad game and the pitch is muddy or bumpy. You won't be able to give the ball to me quickly enough.' He was right, too. When the conditions are bad the really skilful guys can still do their tricks. In circumstances like that, I would win it and let them take it on from there.

The serious injury to Bobby Collins in our first game in European competition was a real sickener to us all, but injuries are part and parcel of the game and we had to take it in our stride. With Gilesy looking as though he was born to the midfield scheming role, Leeds United showed themselves once again to be a real emerging force in the game. Like it or not – and many didn't – Leeds United were here to stay.

We went out of the FA Cup in the fourth round, beaten 1–0 away at Chelsea, and we lost interest in the League Cup at the second-round stage after Revie fielded a weakened side at home to West Bromwich Albion. That game marked the first-team debut of seventeen-year-old goalkeeper David Harvey, who seven years later became first choice at Elland Road and went on to gain international honours with Scotland.

With his team selection, the Gaffer had made it clear that he wasn't interested in the League Cup. The First Division championship was our priority but although we made another great attempt to win it, we had to settle for second place again. We had beaten Liverpool at Anfield by the only goal of the game, scored early on by Peter Lorimer, but Bill Shankly's boys got their revenge the very next day when they travelled to Elland Road and won 1–0. That dented our hopes of taking the title and Liverpool went on to become worthy winners of the championship, with a six-point margin.

While trying to keep pace with the men from Anfield, our first European campaign was gathering momentum. For the second round we had to travel behind the Berlin wall to what was then Communist-controlled East Germany to play SC Leipzig. The weather in Leipzig in late November was inhospitable to say the least. An icy wind was blowing and the pitch was covered with rolled snow and loose ice. It was barely playable and we slipped about all over the place. They were more used to those conditions than we were but somehow we managed to come out of that first leg with a 2–1 advantage. Peter Lorimer and Billy Bremner scored our goals. When the Leipzig players arrived in England for the second leg they were greeted by familiar conditions and on a snow-covered Elland Road pitch they held us to a goalless draw. They were a hard, tough side and we had our work cut out to get the better of them.

Valencia were our next opponents and we might have been better taking some boxing gloves on to the pitch at Elland Road because quite a fight developed. I am the first one to admit that the Leeds side I played in were no angels but Valencia were something else. There had been a lot of ill feeling in the game and it boiled over fifteen minutes from the end when their keeper resented a challenge from Jack and threw a punch at him. A fight broke out between the pair of them, one of their players joined in and that started a right old set-to. The police had to come on to the pitch to separate us all and the referee took both teams to the dressing rooms to calm down. He sent off two of their players and Jack as well. For the record, the first leg ended 1–1, with Peter Lorimer getting our goal after Valencia had taken an early lead. We grabbed a 1–0 win in Valencia and duly progressed to the quarter-finals.

The Hungarian side Ujpest Dozsa, or 'Upsi-Daisy' as Jack called them, were our opponents and despite them having half a dozen internationals in their side, we beat them 4–1 on a quagmire of a pitch at Elland Road. In the second leg in Budapest, we survived a terrific battering to draw 1–1 and so – cock-a-hoop – qualified for the semi-finals. In our first attempt on Europe we had endured some tough physical encounters and proved we could match anyone for effort and aggression – but we got a rude awakening when we came up against Real Zaragoza.

What a fine side they turned out to be! We came away from Spain having lost the first leg 1–0 and summoned up all our energies to beat them 2–1 in the return at Elland Road. Albert Johanneson and Jack Charlton scored our goals. With the aggregate score level at 2–2, the choice of venue for the third game depended on the spin of a coin and we all whooped with delight when Billy Bremner won the toss.

They had five very good forwards in Canaris, Santos, Marcellino, Villa and Lapetia – the magnificent five as they were referred to in the press. We were into May and this was the game when Revie had the pitch watered. We had the fire brigade in at six on the morning of the game to drench the ground because the Spaniards were not supposed to be able to play on a wet surface. It rained heavily, too, and Zaragoza moaned a bit before the game about the state of the pitch. They needn't have bothered – they put three goals past us in the first quarter of an hour and the game was as good as over. We just didn't see which way they went. Jack Charlton pulled one back ten minutes from the end but we were well beaten. They were absolutely superb.

I revelled in those European nights at Elland Road. They were magical as far as I was concerned. Facing players I had never seen or, in many cases, even heard of was a challenge I really enjoyed. A lot of the European sides in those days, while being good in attack, weren't very good defensively and we found we could beat some of them fairly easily. However, against the really good sides, such as Real Zaragoza, it was a different story and it was brilliant to play against such teams.

For our first two seasons in the top division our achievements were fantastic, but having been runners-up in the championship twice, beaten Cup finalists and losing in a European semi-final, we began to wonder if there was some sort of jinx on us. We were almost there but not quite – the nearly men, you might say, and people were beginning to write about us in that way. 'Always the bridesmaid never the bride' was one headline we had to endure. Over the years, we won a fair number of top honours but looking at the talented players we had in the side, we really should have won more. I am often asked why we didn't and I think it was probably the fact that Revie kept us on a tight rein for a long time. Maybe we would have been better had he allowed us more leeway in what we did.

If you ask players of my era what they hated most about being a professional footballer, it's a safe bet that they will say the amount of travelling they had to do. For example, when we went to Leipzig for our second-round tie in the Inter Cities Fairs Cup, it took us eleven hours to get there. Travelling so much and staying in hotels every week can be boring. When we played in Europe, often we would travel on the Monday for a Wednesday game, return on Thursday, have Thursday night at home and then stay away on Friday night for Saturday's game. In fact, you weren't at home very often during the season.

Having been a player himself, Revie was well aware of the boredom this regime could induce, so he introduced carpet bowls and bingo. We had many a laugh but carpet bowls became very competitive. Some of the lads could play the game very well but others were hopeless at it. Johnny Giles was one of the best players and Billy wasn't bad, either. He had a knack of being able to pull off seemingly impossible shots at crucial periods in a game, just like he could on the football field. David Harvey was a dab hand at it and I was OK.

To make it more interesting we used to run a book on the games. Herbert Warner, a friend of Don Revie's and of most of the Leeds lads at that time, would lay the odds. Everyone took part. There was no 'I'm not playing, I'm going to bed'. If you were knocked out early, you would stand around to cheer, especially if you had money riding on a certain pair. Terry Cooper was my partner at bowls and also my room-mate. The lads would each put a fiver in and the winners got the pot but you could also bet on yourself or others if you wanted. The Gaffer used to encourage generous odds so that everyone would have a bet. Such was our interest in carpet bowls that we tended to judge the hotels we stayed in on the suitability of the room they made available to us and the quality of the carpet.

The Gaffer never won because he wanted the lads to win and he was the same when we played cards. More often than not he played in a school with Billy and Jack and he would let them, or whoever he happened to be playing with, win because he thought that would leave the lads on a high. When we played bingo we played for a line and then a house. Terry Cooper was lucky and used to win a few quid but I was just the opposite. I never seemed to win. I don't suppose carpet bowls or bingo would hold much appeal these days but we loved them and they held the boredom at bay. When he became England manager, Revie tried to introduce carpet bowls to the England squad but it never caught on.

The Gaffer's attention to detail was amazing. He never forgot anything. If your wife was ill or had a baby, flowers would arrive at your house for her. I remember him saying to our wives and girlfriends before a Cup final, 'Right ladies, I've had your partners away from home so much during the season, you can treat your-selves to what you want, do what you want and go where you want. Anything you want in the hotel is on me.' He must have thought that was one way of making up for our absences but really he loved to keep us away from them. He was one of those managers who thought sex before a game might not be benefi-cial to his players, so he did his utmost to keep us away from it before games. More than that, he liked to have us all together. It was the family thing. We were the family and he was at the head of it, bonding us into a team in every sense of the word, not just on the pitch but off it as well. It didn't go down too well with a few of the lads but you couldn't knock him for doing what he thought was best for the team and the club. He often went to great lengths to keep us together and away from the girls.

After European games, he would get some drinks in and gather us together to talk about football, but he had kept us on such a tight rein in the build-up that all the lads wanted to do was go out and have a drink in the town. I don't think you could blame us for that. Eventually, and reluctantly, he did allow us to go out after European away games but he always booked the flight home for early the following morning so that we wouldn't stay out too late.

When we played at home, we stayed at the Craiglands Hotel in Ilkley the night before the match – there was a good carpet there for our bowls tournaments. One Easter, when we used to play three games in the space of a few days, Sue, in common with some of the other wives, brought our two children, Michael and Claire, to Ilkley to have Sunday afternoon tea with us. I was relieved to find that my kids still recognised me!

Whatever people might have thought of Revie, his man-

management skills were good. He was strong and at times single-minded but he rarely lost his temper with his players. It just wasn't his style to walk about shouting and bawling, hurling cups across the dressing room or kicking things around. He was strict, though, and you had to do things his way. What he used to do when he was angry was go to the mirror and comb his hair with some very vigorous strokes. It's a wonder he didn't yank clumps of hair out of his head. Then he would say in a most serious manner, 'I'll see you all on Monday,' and walk out of the dressing room. We knew he was annoyed but he never really told us off on the Monday, either. I recall Gary Sprake making a costly error against Crystal Palace. The Gaffer didn't say anything to Gary but made his point by tapping his boots against the dressing-room wall. We ended up drawing that game 1–1 but we should have won. Gary took his eye off the ball and let in a cross that should have been a routine catch.

Punctuality was one of the Gaffer's pet things. On one occasion, I arrived five minutes late at the Mansion House in Roundhay Park for pre-match preparation. It was only just after eleven o'clock when I dashed in but there he was, sitting by the door. He looked at me and glowered at his watch. He didn't say a word but he didn't have to. I was never late again after that.

7

FITNESS TESTS, TIME WASTING AND REVIE'S FORESIGHT

ALL PROFESSIONAL footballers play at some stage or other during a season when not fully fit. In my time we often carried injuries that present-day players would not be allowed to play with. Care of players now is much more scientific than it was years ago. The so-called magic sponge and bucket of water as instant cures for knocks and strains are long since gone, thank goodness, replaced by the very latest in medical treatment. Such advances are to be applauded but I have to smile to myself every time I hear players moan about being tired or stressed-out by the pressure of competition and the number of games they have to play. I was often tired when I was playing but I never made a song and dance about it because, tired or not, all I wanted to do was get out on the field and play football – and in Don Revie we had a manager who was adept at making you feel the injury you had was not as serious as it actually was.

Revie's players never failed fitness tests unless they had a chronic injury. He would put his arm around you and say, 'Come on, son, you can play for me,' and more often than not we did.

Once, both my ankles were so swollen you could not see the ankle bones. On the Saturday morning of a game, the Gaffer rang up and told me to get to Elland Road for a try out. As I struggled out of bed, Sue said to me, 'Where do you think you're going? You can't possibly play with those ankles.'

'The Gaffer wants me to have a try out this morning,' I replied. 'Don't worry, love, I'll not be playing but I have to go to the ground for a test.'

She thought that was stupid and I didn't think I'd a cat in hell's chance of playing that afternoon. When I got there I had some strapping put on both ankles but then had difficulty getting my boots on.

'I'm struggling, Gaffer,' I protested.

'Relax and just try it,' he replied.

I managed to stand up and he asked, 'How is it son?'

'Well, er, it's not so bad, Gaffer.'

'Once you've made a couple of tackles you'll be fine,'

'Yes,' I said. 'It's feeling better already. OK Gaffer, I'll play.'

I kept the strapping on and played.

I cannot understand the modern trend when managers leave players out of the side so they can rest. That would have been foreign to my nature. I would far rather have played. Having to come to terms with the rotation system that some managers insist upon these days would have driven me crackers. I went through five consecutive seasons without missing a single game, including European matches. Clubs didn't have squads as big as they have today, so we played more games.

I only ever failed a fitness test once and that was when I had knee ligament damage. Even then the Gaffer persuaded me to try a tackle, but Les Cocker caught me on the foot, my leg twisted and I was in agony. I told the Gaffer that was it. I couldn't play. He muttered something, walked away and didn't speak to me for three days. He was unbelievable really. Billy Bremner once played when he had a hairline fracture in his leg and, on another occasion, he had to carry on in a match after damaging his knee ligaments. Jack Charlton was shouting to the bench, 'Get him off, he's struggling,' but the call fell on deaf ears, whether by design or not I don't know.

The Gaffer liked to pick the same team all the time. He liked continuity and he did all he could to keep us all playing. Once, when I had a bad back and didn't think I could play, the Gaffer again told me to get down to the ground early on match day. When I arrived he was waiting for me. He took me into the treatment room where Les gave me a painkilling injection.

'You should be all right now,' said the Gaffer. I got up off the bed.

'You're right,' I said. 'I feel a lot better already,' and I went out and played.

Later he told me that Les hadn't injected me with a painkiller at all. He was, as I say, a very persuasive man.

Revie was a manager ahead of his time in a number of ways although he was heavily criticised by the media for some of the things he introduced. The dossiers Syd Owen and Maurice Lindley wrote up on opponents were meticulously compiled and no detail however small was left out. I've known it take nearly an hour for the Gaffer to read them out at team meetings, which he did with due seriousness. We were told if a player got the ball in a certain situation he was likely to do this or that or the other. He would go through every player in the opposition and you sat there thinking yes, yes until boredom took over and it was a struggle to stay awake. We thought it was normal to have dossiers on the opposition. We thought every club did it. They didn't, of course, certainly not to the extent that we did.

A tactic we used when we wanted to kill a bit of time just before the end of a game was to take the ball to the corner flag and invite the opposition to come and get it off us. It wasted time when the game was nearly over and our players were skilful enough to hold on to the ball, but we were lambasted by the media for it. Time wasting is accepted as part of the game now. We could also keep possession for quite a spell when it suited us, for which we were booed. Now teams get applauded for doing it but in the late sixties it wasn't the done thing. We were the first.

The Gaffer used to say to us that if we had a throw-in when the final seconds of the match were ticking away we should throw the ball up the line so that if the opposition got a header it would invariably go out of play again and we would have another throw-in. This is what teams do now all the time but on one occasion against Southampton at the Dell with a couple of minutes to go, I picked one up and automatically threw infield instead of up the line. We lost possession and they went down the other end, crossed the ball and someone knocked it into our net. We had to settle for a draw instead of a win. This time the Gaffer lost his rag and he let me have it with both barrels.

Another tactic we took a lot of criticism for was having Jack Charlton stand on the goalline whenever we got a corner or a free kick in a dangerous place. It came about quite by accident in a practice session. Eddie Gray was curling in corner kicks from the right and Peter Lorimer was doing the same from the left, so Jack decided to make a nuisance of himself by standing right on the goalline directly in front of the goalkeeper so he

Playing for England was always a great thrill for me and here I'm in typically
determined action.

England's 1966 World Cup squad. *Left to right, back row*: Harold Shepherdson (trainer), Les Cock (trainer), Roger Hunt, Ron Flowers, Peter Bonetti, Ron Springett, Gordon Banks, Bobby Moore, Jimmy Greaves and Alf Ramsey (team manager). *Middle row*: Jimmy Armfield, Ian Callaghan, Gerry Byrne, George Eastham, Geoff Hurst, Jack Charlton, Alan Ball and Nobby Stiles. *Front row*: me, George Cohen, Terry Paine, Ray Wilson, Bobby Charlton, Martin Peters and John Connelly.

I scored two goals for England and this was one of them, against Spain in the European Cup of Nations match in Madrid in May 1968, which England won 2–1.

ld Cup Mexico 1970. Brian Labone, Peter Bonetti, me, Bobby Charlton (behind), Bobby
ore, Alan Mullery and Martin Peters pictured at the England team's headquarters in
dalajara.

d a lot of respect for Sir Alf Ramsey and here he is chatting to me and my Leeds
n-mate Paul Madeley at a training session in 1974.

Controversy raged at Elland Road during a match with West Bromwich Albion after referee Ray Tinkler (seen on the right) allowed this goal to stand. Tony Brown (here passing the ball across the face of our goal) was well offside when he intercepted a pass from me just inside our half of the field. Although he was flagged offside he was allowed to run on but even when he passed the ball, Jeff Astle, out of picture, was offside as he hit it into our net.

Feelings were running high and I made mine known to Jeff Astle.

…ree Tinkler is left in no doubt about what Billy Bremner thinks while Albion's John Kaye …6) tries to calm things down.

…s were chasing hard after the title and a defeat by Albion would seriously dent our …ces, a fact that wasn't lost on some of our supporters who invaded the pitch.

One of our most notable successes was in the final of the 1971 Fairs Cup when we beat Juventus on the away goals rule after a 3–3 aggregate score. Mick Bates, seen here in action in the Elland Road leg, had scored one of our goals in the first leg.

Here we are with the trophy. Don Revie is on the right of the picture and I'm second from left at the back.

Gaffer leads us out at Wembley for the 1972 Centenary FA Cup final while Bertie Mee is
e head of the Arsenal side. I'm fifth in the Leeds line behind Billy Bremner, David Harvey,
Reaney and Johnny Giles. We won the game 1–0 to bring the FA Cup back to Elland
l for the first time.

great feeling to win such a coveted
y and here I'm celebrating our
vement with goalkeeper David Harvey.

Mick Jones suffered a dislocated elbow just before
the end of the game and he was in a lot of pain as
I helped him up the steps to receive his medal
from the Queen. Here we're on our way down.

Clenched fist salute. It's my way of urging myself and everyone else to give everything for the cause.

Well done, Norm! I receive the congratulations of my Leeds team-mates after I scored against Southampton at the Dell in May 1973 – but the Saints beat us 3–1.

couldn't see the ball coming over. He did it in knockabout sessions with England, too. Goalkeepers had had nothing like that to deal with before. Gary Sprake didn't like it one bit and we reasoned that if he found it a nuisance, so would all the other keepers. It was a legitimate tactic and we used it to good effect. Jack got quite a few goals from it. Unsurprisingly, the press had a right go at us but it couldn't have been a bad tactic because a lot of teams followed our example.

Of course, we bent the rules to suit our needs but a lot occurred in games then that would never be tolerated these days. Referees allowed much greater physical contact than players are allowed now. The game was not as fast as it is today and no quarter was given or asked. You accepted it as part and parcel of the game and I think the fans liked to see a bit of 'needle'. In my opinion, if you take away the physical contact the game suffers. I made my presence felt with some hefty tackles and while I steamed in fearlessly I never did so with the intention of hurting an opponent. At one time I was referred to as the hardest man in football. I certainly wasn't that. In fact, I'm a bit of a softy really. There were others I could name who were just as tough as I was and more so. If a ball was there to be won it was my job to try to win it. Not every tackle I made was a fair one because it is impossible to time every tackle to perfection. I got into all sorts of scrapes during my career and I was sent off a few times but I never had it in mind to injure a player deliberately. Things happen in the heat of the moment but nothing was premeditated.

However, one tackle I made was quite horrendous. It was on John Craven of Crystal Palace and it was really stupid. I caught him with my right foot of all things, which was the one I usually used for standing on! I never meant to hurt him – and I don't believe I did – but it looked nasty and I got booked for it. That was probably the worst one of my career. I regretted it straight away and was suitably repentant, apologising as I picked him up. While he was down he grinned at me and we both knew he was all right. There was a bit of anger and frustration in that tackle because he had knocked me about a couple of times and wound me up. There had been a bit of 'needle' between us. I was pleased to see that he played in Palace's next game.

Little vendettas developed over the years but I very rarely lost my temper on the field. I was not usually that type of person. I was actually quite friendly. I had a habit of putting my arm round referees' shoulders whenever they pulled me up for some indiscretion, but I wasn't aware I was doing it until someone pointed it out to me. If it got me out of a few bookings, all well and good, but I never tried to con the referee.

There are two ways of looking at being a hard man. I was aware of what was going on in a game and saw danger coming. I still went into the tackle but I used to protect myself accordingly. The real hard men were those who went into challenges without even sensing danger or caring how they might end up. They were truly fearless. We had a lad at Leeds in the very early days of my playing career by the name of Willie Bell and he was one of the bravest men I have seen in my life. He never blinked, he never flinched, he just went for it.

There have been lots of really hard players who fall into this category. Southampton's George Kirby was one and Burnley's Andy Lochhead was another. We used to call him Bald Eagle because he was great in the air and was going thin on top. What a great centre-forward he was and at one stage Leeds actually tried to buy him. I thought Ron Yeats at Liverpool was exceptionally tough and physical while David Harvey was one of the bravest goalkeepers I ever saw. He would dive headfirst at the feet of inrushing forwards. Whether that was bravery or stupidity I'm not sure but it was beyond the call of duty.

When I was playing we always regarded the first tackle as what you might call a 'freebie'. Referees very rarely booked you so early in a game. The Gaffer used to say to me, 'Norman, when your man gets the ball for the first time, let him know you're there. Hit him hard and let him know you're on his case.' I didn't disappoint him on that one. Even Alf Ramsey, when he was manager of England, used to say to me in his posh voice, 'Norman, you do what you have to do.' To my mind he was saying the same as Revie. The idea was that if you hit your opponent hard enough in that first encounter, he might well be glancing over his shoulder every time he got the ball, wondering when he was going to get a bit more of the rough stuff. If your opponent backed off, it made your afternoon a very easy one. If he refused to be intimidated, when you got the ball you expected him to hit you just as hard as you had hit him and if that was the case, you had no cause for complaint. Some forwards didn't like the physical stuff. Jimmy Greaves was a great goalscorer, one of the very best, but he didn't relish the rough stuff and he couldn't tackle a hot dinner. As far as I was concerned, I couldn't have played the game any other way. At professional level, it just had to be competitive.

Four of us were labelled as hard men – Nobby Stiles, Tommy Smith and Ron 'Chopper' Harris being the other three. The only naturally tough one of the four was Tommy, lovely fella that he is. The rest of us were fairly laid back off the field. There was one occasion, though, during my England career when I came close to playing the hard man off the field. I read an article by a London-based journalist in which he said I wasn't fit to grace the Wembley turf. He used to have a 'pop' at Leeds on a regular basis but we had a lot of criticism from the media and generally took no notice. However, I took exception to being labelled not fit to grace Wembley and after one England game, when he asked me a question, I just walked away because if I'd stayed I might have got a little bit too angry. People can criticise you and, like it or not, you have to put up with it. Normally I did but I thought that particular comment about me was, for the want of a better expression, over the top!

There were exceptions but I don't think too many of the London journalists cared overmuch for Revie. Yet he was a manager who thought very deeply about the game. Another area in which he was ahead of his time was nutrition. To start with, when we travelled the day before a game, we would eat whatever we wanted to that evening. In London, we would stay at the Royal Garden Hotel. They had a very well stacked hors d'oeuvres trolley and we used to raid that and follow on with soup, a main course and dessert, and we'd think nothing of ordering something to eat in our rooms at about 10.30. Gluttons? Probably, but we didn't see it that way. We were fit young lads and it didn't seem to bother us at all. Before a home game we would always eat steak and chips, which I really enjoyed. All of a sudden the Gaffer did away with that sort of thing. He began to think about carbohydrates years before people in sport took nutrition seriously. We went on to boiled chicken and beans and he used to hand out Mars bars to give us energy. At his insistence we would take our own food with us to some European games, in case those countries didn't have the type of food we were used to or, for that matter, wanted. Eventually, everyone jumped on the bandwagon yet he never got any credit for it. Now leading clubs employ nutritionists, sports psychologists, sprint coaches and goodness knows what else.

When he was manager of England, Revie obtained sponsorship for the national team, bringing in Admiral, the sportswear company, but he got some terrible stick from the press for doing that. I think they thought that obtaining commercial gain from the England set-up was just not done, but look at England now. They make an absolute fortune out of sponsorship.

We never got too many injuries, which was surprising because it was a physical game and we played it that way. The Gaffer always wanted to put his main team out but sometimes he had to make changes, even though he hated having to do so. When Johnny Giles got a knock he brought in Mick Bates and when Eddie Gray missed games with thigh and shoulder injuries, Paul Madeley was called up. It was fortunate that we had Paul because we could stick him in anywhere and he would do a fine job for the team. In my view, his best position was alongside the centre-half – where I played! – or at right-back. I could have been out on my ear and I was lucky that Paul was so adept at playing anywhere. Another thing going for me was that I was left-footed while Paul wasn't. If he or I had been better in the air, ours would probably have been the next central defensive partnership at Leeds, when Jack Charlton left. We did play together and we could do it, but not as a permanent thing. Neither of us was a good enough header of the ball for that.

I was always labelled one-footed and I couldn't argue with that but I did well enough on my trusted left foot. It served me well throughout my career. Funnily enough, I'm right-handed. The only other thing I did left-handed was play snooker.

When I signed professional forms for Leeds, the Gaffer, who was very keen on golf, told me that either I played the game or I had to act as a caddie. I thought, 'Well, I ain't caddying for anyone,' so I decided to have a go at playing. I'm glad that I did. If we didn't have a midweek fixture, we would go for a game of golf on the Tuesday and afterwards on to Harrogate baths for a massage. I was the Gaffer's golf partner and we almost always played Johnny Giles and Peter Lorimer, who were both good pressure players, knocking in the putts. The Gaffer and I were not so good and the stick we used to get from them was something else. That was part of it. Taking the mickey out of each other was the real enjoyment, rather than winning a fiver. We had some great times playing golf and I still love the game. My putting's a bit better now.

8

THE WORLD CUP – JOY, EMBARRASSMENT AND SADNESS

Being a member of England's 1966 World Cup winning squad was a great honour of which I was very proud but, sadly, apart from fading memories the only thing of note I have to remind me of that very special time in English football history is a photograph of the England squad taken at Highbury when we wore our best tracksuits. It hangs in my toilet at home. I was absolutely delighted to be selected for the final twenty-two-man squad. There were twenty-six of us initially and we were together for weeks before the finals began. The squad had to be whittled down to twenty-two and as none of us wanted to spoil our chances by stepping out of line we were all models of good behaviour. Nobby Stiles's wife was pregnant and she kept asking him why he couldn't come home to be with her but he kept on saying he couldn't because he didn't want to damage his chances of being selected! That's how keen we all were so that picture of mine has pride of place. It's there for me to look at every day and most people who come to the house visit the downstairs loo, so they see it, too. I got the idea of hanging the picture there after going to a friend's house and noticing that she had pictures in her loo. I thought it was a good idea and did the same.

That photograph and the odd programme provide the only tangible evidence that I was part of the 1966 squad and that rankles with me. Even now, all these years later, I feel that there is something missing. The FA could at least have had replica medals made for those who didn't get a winner's medal – only the eleven who played got a medal – or given us some memento. I don't know if Terry Paine, Ian Callaghan and the others who made the odd appearance got anything but the rest of us certainly didn't. The issue was raised at the time but nothing came of it. I don't know if FIFA rules prevented the FA from having other medals struck but I honestly thought that once the dust had settled on our victory over West Germany in the final, the FA might have done something for us but they didn't. It's sad really, but I don't think it's too late for the FA to think again about this issue. It would be a great gesture on their part, and it would certainly be appreciated, if they could have a replica medal struck for us, or at least something official that we could show our grandchildren to say that we were part of that historic occasion. I may have been on the sidelines but I still kicked every ball, made every challenge and felt every tackle. I was completely wrapped up in it.

Although I didn't get a game in the finals, there seemed at one stage a slight chance that I might. Nobby Stiles, a great competitor if ever there was one, had come in for heavy criticism for the aggressive nature of his play and his tackling, especially in the game against France. One tackle in particular, which put the French forward Jacques Simon out of the game, caused quite a stir. It was a tough challenge, a bad one, and everyone was up in arms about it. Sir Alf Ramsey came under pressure, not least I think from people at the FA, to keep Nobby out of the England side from then on. There were suggestions that he should put me in the team in Nobby's place but Alf, being Alf, stuck to his guns. His job was to win the World Cup and if he thought we had a better chance with Nobby in the team, he would select him and no one would persuade him otherwise. Alf had his plans all laid out and he knew what he was going to do. He was his own man and he refused to bow to any outside pressures. He stood by Nobby, and that turned out to be the right thing to do.

I have already made it clear how much respect and admiration I had for Don Revie and I also developed a great deal of respect for Sir Alf. The two of them were poles apart as people but they had one thing in common – they knew how to get the best out of players and that made them good managers. It's funny but while most people were writing England off, Alf told us from the very start, 'We're going to win this Cup.' These were not just words of encouragement. He really believed it. If I'm honest, though, I don't think that deep down the players did.

We trained at Lilleshall and our first game, against Uruguay, turned out to be pretty grim. The sole aim of the very defensive-minded Uruguayan side seemed to be to try to frustrate us and we managed only a goalless draw. The press got their knives out right away and slaughtered us. I watched the game from the stand along with Jimmy Armfield.

There wasn't a lot happening in our next match, against Mexico, until Bobby Charlton lit the fuse. He latched on to a ball forty yards out, swayed past a couple of defenders, as he used to do, and unleashed a shot from about thirty yards in the inside-right position. The ball screamed into the net and we went on to win that game 2–0, Roger Hunt scoring our second. That was the result that really launched our bid for the coveted trophy. We went to the top of our group with that win and stayed there when we beat France 2–0 in our third game. Hunt scored both our goals, further underlining the belief Alf had in the Liverpool player.

Jimmy Greaves picked up an injury against the French and his appearance in that game was his last in the World Cup. Some thought he was fit to play in our next game, against Argentina, but whether he was or not, Alf decided not to select him. It was well publicised at the time that Jimmy wasn't too pleased at being overlooked and when we were asked to attend a reception some-time later to receive a picture of the winning team, Greavsie was the only one who didn't turn up. There's no denying that he was a very popular player, certainly with the public in London, but Alf again stuck to his guns. He wasn't to be swayed by anyone and he brought in Geoff Hurst, which proved to be a master-stroke. Geoff headed the only goal of the game against Argentina, ten minutes from time, to put us into the semi-finals.

The game against Argentina was a nasty affair and the England players had to put up with some real rough stuff that culminated, towards the end of the first half, with the Argentine captain Antonio Rattin being sent off. It was something like ten minutes before he could be persuaded to leave the field and at one stage I thought the whole team were going to walk off. There was a great deal of ill-feeling in the game and it wasn't the sort of spectacle you wanted in such a prestigious competition. The ill-feeling carried on after the final whistle had blown with Alf refusing to let the England players exchange shirts with the opposition.

In contrast to Argentina, our semi-final opponents, Portugal, had shown a refreshingly positive attitude in their earlier matches. They came into the game against England having scored fourteen goals in four games, with Eusebio having hit half of those. Eusebio, a talented and skilful player, was the man who made Portugal tick and it didn't need a genius to realise that he could be a real danger to England unless he was marked well. Who should get the job? Yes, of course, Nobby Stiles. The potential for an explosive battle between the two of them was clear. Nobby wasn't the sort of player to stand on ceremony but as things turned out he did a sound job on the Portuguese playmaker without the contest between them becoming over-heated or unsavoury in any way. Eusebio scored from the penalty spot after Jack Charlton had handled. Two goals from Bobby Charlton gave us the win and put England into our first ever World Cup final. It was a wonderful feeling, of course, and the critics had to eat their words.

Alf was not to be moved for the final and again overlooked a fit Greaves. We suffered a blow when Haller put West Germany ahead after about quarter of an hour but Geoff Hurst equalised five minutes later before Martin Peters put us 2–1 up only for Weber to square the match again. Extra time followed and, of course, Hurst bagged another two goals to give England the coveted Jules Rimet Trophy.

Controversy surrounded the first of those extra-time goals and the debate about whether the ball actually crossed the line when it bounced down from the crossbar still goes on to this day. I couldn't see from where I was sitting but the referee decided that it had and that's all that mattered.

The official celebration banquet was held at the Royal Garden Hotel in Kensington and the wives and girlfriends of the players were invited. I was there on my own because Susie, whom I married two years later, didn't want to go. In fact, she turned down the chance to attend the final as well. Ian Callaghan, I think, was the only other player who didn't have a partner with him. Susie has never been that interested in football and I don't think she has ever regretted missing it. All the same, it would have been nice for her to have been there.

As far as I was concerned, though, it was great to be part of it all but I have to admit that when the final whistle blew it was something of an anti-climax for me, and on a personal level I also found it embarrassing. Alf had said that at the final whistle he wanted the whole twenty-two man squad to go out on to the pitch, irrespective of whether we had won or not. It was his way of letting the fans know that we appreciated their backing. Those of us who were watching from the stand had been told that we should leave our seats before the end of the game and get down into the tunnel so that we would be ready as soon as the referee ended the game. England were winning 2–1 when Jimmy Armfield and I left our seats, upstairs in the stand. We headed for the lift but there was a little bit of a delay and when we eventually got to the tunnel we saw the band assembled and ready to march out on to the pitch. Then we were told Germany had equalised so we watched the extra-time period from the England bench. It was a great relief when we finally won and, just as Alf had ordered, we all walked out on to the pitch to salute the victory and the crowd, which I found rather awkward. I was wearing a suit and tie and had not played in the game yet there I was, milking the cheers of an adoring crowd. I hadn't even kicked a ball in the warm-up.

The bonus for winning the World Cup was £2,000 for each

of the eleven who played in the final but they voted to share it among the squad, so we actually received £1,000 each before tax. If it hadn't been for the team spirit in the squad and the generosity of the eleven who played in the final, the rest of us would have got nothing at all in the way of a bonus.

Alf made every one of us in the squad feel very much part of things. It wasn't a case of the eleven who played and the rest of us. There was no division. We were all together as a unit. He saw to that. We were all made to feel important. I thought he was a smashing man, although I knew I was never going to play that many games for him because I was up against Bobby Moore and I was never going to replace Bobby on a permanent basis. I realised the only chance I had of getting a game was if Bobby was injured or rested and that wasn't very often. Nevertheless, I was always keen to go with England because it was my country and because of Alf. I respected him as a person and as a manager. Like Don Revie, he never really raised his voice, even when things went wrong, but he had the total and utter respect of the lads. You knew where you stood with Alf so you didn't overstep the line. He was a very polite man and as we prepared to return home after matches, he would always make a point of saying to me, 'Oh, thanks for coming, Norman. Lovely to see you. See you again for the next international.' He was forever the gentleman – I had a lot of time for him.

Much as I loved being a part of the England team, it was usually a battle for me to get there in the first place. Don Revie would do everything he could to stop me. He liked his team to stay together. He even offered to pay me the fee I would get for being with England if I would stay away. I can't remember just what the fee was but it can't have been that much. In any case,

I used to say to him, 'Gaffer, if you don't mind, I'm going.' After all, I was proud to be selected for the England squad. Even though I had to play second fiddle to Bobby Moore, I regarded it as an honour and I wanted to go. I was first asked to attend the group sessions in 1965 when I wasn't all that old and in awe of those around me. I was rubbing shoulders with the best players England had – Bobby Charlton, Gordon Banks, Jimmy Greaves. I was young and inexperienced but I loved it. I used to tell the Gaffer that I wouldn't be playing but he still didn't like it because he knew I would be away from Elland Road and would miss out on training at the club. He tried it on with everyone and some of the Scottish lads didn't always go off with Scotland. I went with England for nine years from 1965 until shortly after the Gaffer got the England job.

9

THREE GOOD
SEASONS AND
TROPHIES AT LAST

ALTHOUGH Leeds were a good side, we had our share of disappointments and season 1966–67 brought one or two of those our way, not to mention one particular result that was a real shock to the system. We had to settle for fourth place in the championship behind Manchester United, Nottingham Forest and Tottenham, we reached the final of the Inter Cities Fairs Cup and lost an FA Cup semi-final to Chelsea in controversial circumstances, but it was our defeat in the fourth round of the League Cup that really rocked us. Having beaten Newcastle and Preston, we went down 7–0 to West Ham at Upton Park and that was a real embarrassment. We weren't used to losing let alone being thumped like that.

Two days before the West Ham tie we had beaten Arsenal 1–0 in a league game at Highbury, with a fluke goal from Jack. The Gaffer had changed our system for that game – Willie Bell, who normally played left-back, picked up George Graham in midfield and I was pushed to left-back. The win wasn't convincing by any means. We stayed in London for the League Cup match. I was rooming with Johnny Giles and we both hoped the Gaffer would not play the same system for the Cup game. Unfortunately, he did. He put me to left-back and told Bell to do a man-marking job on Geoff Hurst.

I was up against Peter Brabrook – a flying machine – and he just tormented the life out of me. He simply flew past me almost at will. Johnny Sissons scored in the first minute and completed his hat-trick in thirty-five minutes – it was one of the finest hat-tricks I have ever seen – and John 'Budgie' Byrne destroyed Jack. He kept getting round the back of him. Bobby Moore got possession and laid off the ball time and again, and we came off at half-time four goals down. The daft thing was that although we had been battered, we actually felt that we still had a chance of winning the tie. The Gaffer swapped things around, putting me back in the middle and Willie Bell at left-back, but we were in disarray. At the end, Geoff Hurst had scored three and Martin Peters got another to complete the rout.

People reading the results in the newspapers the following day probably thought it was a misprint. It was Leeds United's heaviest defeat since losing 8–1 at Stoke in 1934. Young David Harvey had come in as goalkeeper and the poor lad didn't have a chance. I remember thinking there was very little he could have done about it. West Ham were on fire that night.

We'd got over that shock by the time we embarked on the FA Cup trail, comfortably disposing of Crystal Palace and West Bromwich in home ties and scoring eight goals in the process. When the draw for the fifth round was made we found ourselves up against our old adversary, Sunderland. It took three meetings and 300 minutes of football to settle it. The first game at Roker Park ended 1–1, with Jack getting our equaliser, and we drew again in the replay at Elland Road. Johnny Giles scored two minutes after John O'Hare had put Sunderland ahead. A huge crowd turned out for that game. The turnstiles had to be closed half-an-hour before kick-off with thousands of people locked out. Crowd numbers in the stadium are recorded at 57, 892 but it was thought that quite a lot more people climbed in over the walls. Under pressure from that record crowd, a barrier gave way on the Lowfields Road terraces and some twenty people were injured, fortunately not seriously. The match was held up for fifteen minutes before an agreement between the police and the match referee, Ray Tinkler, allowed it to continue with hundreds of fans sitting on the ground near the touchlines.

In the second reply at Hull City's Boothferry Park ground, Rod Belfitt put us ahead very early on and we held that lead until ten minutes or so from the end when Alan Gauden got an equaliser for Sunderland. With a minute to go we were awarded a penalty when Cec Irwin was adjudged to have fouled Jimmy Greenhoff. I don't remember much about the incident itself now but Sunderland were certainly irate about the penalty decision and had George Mulhall and George Herd sent off in the aftermath of the award. Gilesy slotted the penalty away and we were through to the semis.

The matches were coming thick and fast. We stayed in Hull overnight and flew to Italy the following morning for our Fairs Cup game against Bologna. In my opinion, the reason why we failed to pick up a trophy that season was that there was no time for any rest. The game against Bologna was our fifth in twelve days. When you think about it, we must have got on well because we were living in each other's pockets for an awfully long time.

Manchester City were our opponents in the FA Cup quarter-finals and we overcame them with the help of another goal from Jack. Then it was on to Villa Park to play Chelsea in the semi-finals and we fell headlong into controversy again. We had maybe been a little fortunate to beat Sunderland, but our luck was definitely out against the boys from Stamford Bridge. They scored through Tony Hateley a minute before half-time but we thought we had equalised a couple of minutes from the end when Terry Cooper struck but the referee disallowed his effort. To cap it all, Peter Lorimer had one ruled out just after that because the referee, Ken Burns, said Chelsea's defensive wall was not ten yards away when the free kick was taken. In effect, he punished us for the failings of the opposition. The ball had been quickly rolled to Peter and he lashed a real screamer into the net. A big fuss was made about that decision but the referee remained unmoved. That bad decision robbed us of a return to Wembley, which pleased those of our critics who delighted in our failure to win a trophy.

We had made encouraging progress in the Fairs Cup, beating DWS Amsterdam 8–2 on aggregate and Valencia 3–1 on aggregate to qualify for the fourth-round tie against Bologna. A fine defensive display restricted the Italians to one goal in the first game. We would have liked an away goal, of course, but we felt we had done a good job in keeping it to 1–0. We knew the home game wouldn't be easy. Johnny Giles put us ahead from the penalty spot after just eight minutes but that was as good as it got. We couldn't get another but we kept a clean sheet and as the aggregate scores were level at 1–1 the tie had to be decided on the spin of a red and green disc. As captain of the visitors, Giacomo Bulgarelli had the call and he called red. Fortunately for us, the disc came down green. It was a tough way for Bologna to go out of the competition.

We faced Scottish opposition in the semi-finals, Kilmarnock making the trip to Elland Road for the first leg. Rod Belfitt came in at centre-forward for Jimmy Greenhoff, who was injured, and enjoyed one of the finest half-hours of his career. Rod was part of Revie's squad but often had to be content with a background role. On this occasion, though, he was given the job of leading the front line and he scored after two minutes, put us two up in the fourth and completed his hat-trick on the half-hour – sensational stuff. Johnny Giles added our fourth goal from the penalty spot and while we were very happy at scoring four we weren't too pleased about letting Kilmarnock score twice to reduce our advantage. All six goals were scored in an action-packed first half in front of a crowd of 43,000. As a defender, I hated us to concede goals in any game – friendly or otherwise. It was my job to stop the opposition from scoring and that was in my mind throughout every game.

The game at Kilmarnock couldn't have been in greater contrast to the first leg as neither side found the net, so we went through to the final on a 4–2 aggregate score. The final, against Dinamo Zagreb, was held over to the beginning of the 1967–68 season and we travelled to Zagreb for the first leg without Johnny Giles, Paul Madeley, Willie Bell and Albert Johanneson. Even though we lost the game 2–0 we felt we could pull it round in the return match but despite an all-out attacking effort we couldn't pierce their solid defence and we had to settle for a goalless draw.

A long and involved season had finished, yet again, without a trophy. The media loved it, saying we were never going to win anything. That was annoying because for a young – and some might say naive – side we hadn't done too badly. The turnstiles at Elland Road were ringing, although the money didn't filter down to the players. In reality, we'd had a good season. What wouldn't Leeds United give for a season such as that now? I think it shows just how high the standards we set for ourselves were in the late 1960s.

It wasn't long before we were pulling on our boots for the 1967–68 campaign. Again we were battling on four fronts – Europe, the League and our two domestic Cup competitions. We had a fairly trouble-free route to the League Cup final, beating Luton Town and Bury in the first two rounds, both at Elland Road, before we set off to meet our old adversaries, Sunderland, at Roker Park. This time we got through reasonably unscathed, two goals from Jimmy Greenhoff giving us a 2–0 success. Billy Bremner and Peter Lorimer scored to beat Stoke City and put us into the semi-final against Derby County. Brian Clough was manager of Derby at the time and he had his team fully prepared for our first-leg visit to the Baseball Ground. He didn't like us but we got the better of a very tough encounter and came away with Johnny Giles having scored the only goal of the game from the penalty spot. We celebrated that success by stopping at a local chippie on the way back and ordering fish and chips twenty-eight times. We really knew how to celebrate! The fish fryer had to work overtime on that order but it was a good bit of business for him. When Derby came to Elland Road for the second leg we shaded that game 3–2 with a couple of strikes from Rod Belfitt and a goal from Eddie Gray to go through to the final on a 4–2 aggregate.

We were back at Wembley, this time against Arsenal, three

years after our first appearance at the famous old stadium. As we ran out on to the pitch we spotted a banner, waving at the Leeds end, that read, 'Norman "Bites Yer Legs" Hunter'. It caught the attention of ITV who screened it several times and from that day onwards the nickname stuck with me. I've had to live with it, and the jokes, ever since. You know the sort of thing – 'Norman's come home with a damaged leg. Oh yes, who does it belong to?'

I've often been asked what I thought about the banner when I saw it for the first time but, to be honest, I didn't think much about it. It didn't make me more aggressive and I certainly never thought about trying to live up to the description! I got used to it and even saw the funny side. It helped to keep me in the public eye. Sometime after the final I met the guys who were responsible for the banner at a gym in Horsforth, Leeds, and we had a laugh about it. I also have a permanent reminder in the shape of a bronze statue of a player with a huge bite taken out of his calf, which was presented to me by members of the Bradford branch of the Leeds United Supporters Club. It's not on show because Sue never quite took to it. She didn't like it when I first got it and she doesn't like it now.

There was plenty of opportunity to hoist the banner aloft during the game. Having lost to Liverpool in the 1965 FA Cup final, and still without a trophy to show for our efforts as an improving team in the top flight, the important thing was simply to win the match and the League Cup. Just how we did it we really didn't care. All we had on our minds was beating Arsenal, and Terry Cooper scored a dream goal to settle the match in our favour.

Apparently, Terry had had a dream for three nights running that he would score the winning goal in the final, so it really was a dream come true for him – and for Leeds United. He didn't score many but that was a vital one although I have to admit that we were a little lucky to get away with it. Jack Charlton had stationed himself on the goal line and Paul Madeley had jumped up all over their goalkeeper, Jim Furnell, at a corner kick. Furnell just managed to palm the ball out and it went to Terry, who whacked it with his left foot into the goal.

It was hardly a classic match by any stretch of the imagination. In fact, it was an awful game but we weren't worried about that. We needed a trophy and we had finally got one – mission accomplished. It was important for the team and the club to win a trophy and it was also important for our fans. They were ecstatic and we felt on cloud nine. To have made the breakthrough and put our first major trophy on the shelf was fantastic.

While we were making our way through the League Cup competition, we were also contesting the Inter Cities Fairs Cup. A high-scoring victory over Spora Luxembourg got us off to a flying start. It turned out to be a stroll as we put nine goals past them in the first leg at their place. Peter Lorimer got four of them, Jimmy Greenhoff a couple and there was one each from Billy Bremner, Paul Madeley and Mick Jones. In the return leg, we scored a further seven goals. Albert Johanneson hit a hat-trick, Greenhoff scored twice and Terry Cooper and Peter Lorimer got one each to set up a club record win.

We went on to become the scourge of the Scots as we played three games in a row against opposition from north of the border – Hibs, Rangers and Dundee – and disposed of the lot of them, but I have to admit they weren't easy games. Hibs proved to be very difficult but we managed a 1–0 win at home in the first leg and drew 1–1 at Easter Road. Ibrox is never an easy place to go and we were happy enough with a goalless draw there, and to win 2–0 at Elland Road. A Johnny Giles penalty and a goal from Peter Lorimer saw us through. Paul Madeley's goal gave us a 1–1 draw at Dundee in the first leg of the semi-final and we reached the final after winning 1–0 at Elland Road, courtesy of a strike from Eddie Gray.

For some reason – international fixture demands on players, I think – the final was held over until the 1968–69 season and it was August 1968 when we took on the Hungarian side, Ferencvaros. The first leg at Elland Road was a tough battle. The Hungarians got most of their players behind the ball, hoping to hit us on the break, and we scored the only goal of the game, Mick Jones forcing the ball in from close range. A one-goal lead to take into the second leg a month later was welcome but we knew it would not make for a comfortable ride. The atmosphere in the famous Nep Stadium was electric as 76,000 fans packed in to see the expected fight-back from Ferencvaros, but what they did to us at Elland Road we did to them in Hungary – only we did it better. They threw everything at us but we hoisted a blanket defence and kept them out. We took a rare old battering but Gary Sprake was absolutely magnificent that night. He kept a clean sheet in one of the most outstanding displays I ever saw from him. He was superb.

Sprake was a very good goalkeeper but he was prone to the odd howler or the occasional rush of blood to the head and when a goalkeeper drops a clanger it's usually costly. When our FA Cup run that season ended at the semi-final stage, Joe Royle, playing for Everton, had given Sprake a rough time. In fact, he had been knocking Gary about quite a lot and in one incident when Gary had the ball near the corner of the 18-yard box, Joe came to challenge. Instead of concentrating on the ball, Gary, keen for some retribution, went to try to kick it and Joe at the same time but he mis-kicked the ball and it went straight to Jimmy Husband. He knocked the ball back in towards the goal and Jack Charlton had to handle to prevent it going into our net. There wasn't a lot more Jack could have done but it made no difference really because Johnny Morrissey scored the penalty. That was just before half-time but it was enough to put Everton into the final.

So that season we had to be content with winning the Fairs Cup and the League Cup – and we were. In fact, those two successes came as a great relief to us all. They worked wonders for our confidence as a team and as individuals, and paved the way for the big prize from the 1968–69 campaign. Revie said before the kick-off that he wanted the league championship and we were hell bent on winning it. Cup competitions are exciting, especially for supporters, but the League measures a team's overall ability.

We made a cracking start to the campaign, winning seven and drawing two of our opening nine matches before we lost 3–1 to Manchester City. That season, we lost just two league games, the other being at Burnley. They turned us over 5–1 at Turf Moor. There was a lot of ill-feeling between the two sides and games with them were usually hard battles. An up-and-coming team, they could field such players as Ralph Coates, Steve Kindon and Martin Dobson. In those days, Burnley were renowned for having a first-class youth development policy and most of their players had come through the ranks. Coates was brilliant that day and Kindon ran all over the place. We were well beaten and it dented our pride because we had taken most other things in our stride.

As a defender you take such a result very badly. I certainly did. You don't forget a big defeat like that and we were ready for Burnley when they visited Elland Road later that season. We thrashed them 6–1, Lorimer got two and Bremner, Giles, Jones and Eddie Gray the others. Revenge was sweet.

Our penultimate match of the season was at Liverpool and they were our only remaining rivals for the championship. But while Liverpool needed to win to keep alive their hopes, all we had to do to clinch the title was hold them to a draw. That, however, was easier said than done in those days because Bill Shankly's Liverpool side had turned Anfield into a fortress. Very few visiting teams came away from that ground with much to sing about.

We rarely went anywhere with the sole purpose of defending but this was one occasion when we set our sights on a draw. It was a gamble and a very brave thing to do. I know that we had a reputation for being a defensive team but we were more than that. I cannot remember the Gaffer ever saying that we should go out with the express intention of playing for a draw until this match. Liverpool were a great team and I remember thinking that we would have to soak up a tremendous amount of pressure for ninety minutes.

We knew Liverpool would come at us with all guns blazing and they did. The game wasn't the best as a spectacle but it was played at a very fast pace and we defended superbly. Billy Bremner played as sweeper that night. We adopted spoiling tactics and worked hard at closing Liverpool down quickly. The final few minutes of the game seemed an eternity with the championship almost, but not quite, ours. Then the referee blew the final whistle and Leeds United were the champions for the first time.

My first feeling was one of numbness, followed by great elation. Don Revie had told us before the match that whatever the result we were to walk towards the Kop and salute the Liverpool fans. We were horrified at the thought but the Gaffer insisted. The memory of it still makes the hairs on the back of my neck stand up. As we walked towards the Liverpool fans massed on the Kop there was a deathly silence and then, all of a sudden, a guy was hoisted up on someone's shoulders and he started chanting 'Champions, Champions'. The rest of them picked it up and the chant echoed around the ground. That demonstrated the respect there was between the two teams and the two clubs. It had been a diabolical game and we'd pipped their team for the title yet here they all were chanting for us. I'll never forget it. We always regarded the Liverpool fans as being very knowledgeable about the game. We had restricted their team to hardly any chances and they must have thought we were worthy winners of the title. It was great of them.

We had been close to winning the title a few times without actually landing the big prize. Now we had it and I thought that if any team deserved it, Leeds United did. Not many teams win the championship without deserving to. It's a long haul to get there and teams are tested to the full. It was a great feeling. I cannot recall this particular celebration, however. We had lots of nights out as a team for various reasons – if one of the lads got engaged, or when one of us became a father and so on. We often went out for a few drinks but we never went over the top.

As we concentrated our efforts on the championship we lost out in both the domestic Cup competitions, Sheffield Wednesday beating us in the third round of the FA Cup and Crystal Palace in the League Cup at the fourth-round stage. Our involvement in the Fairs Cup ended at the quarter-final stage when we were beaten by Ujpest Dozsa in a two-leg tie in March but, as we were very much involved in the title race, I don't think Revie was too bothered about that. The title was the coveted prize. Losing twice only – both away from Elland Road – in a forty-two-match league campaign was a tremendous achievement. We hadn't used all that many players either – seventeen it was. At the time, you got two points for a victory and we finished with 67 points, which was a record back then. Had there been three points awarded for a win, we'd have ended the campaign with 94 points. We felt that we had arrived as a top-class team. Deep down we all believed that we were good enough. Having taken the title, we started to think we needed to win the FA Cup. We wanted to win the League again, of course, and continue in Europe, preferably in the European Cup. We were an ambitious bunch and there was no way we were going to rest on our laurels.

10

FIXTURE CONGESTION, FATIGUE AND NO CONSIDERATION

ALTHOUGH the Leeds United side of the late 1960s was very much a home-grown unit – and all the better for that – once we had established ourselves as a force in the English game we relied a great deal on buying a player here and there to improve the side and continue our progress. Don Revie was a master at making the right kind of signing, which was just as well because, successful as we were, as a club we didn't have all that much money to throw around in the transfer market. The manager had to be spot on and, usually, he was. He had proved himself to be a good judge of a player in the early days when he was striving to put the club on an even keel and then climb out of the old Second Division. Bobby Collins, Alan Peacock and Johnny Giles were great buys and the Gaffer again proved himself in the transfer market. Of course, it helps to have a good scouting network and Syd Owen, Maurice Lindley and Tony Collins were all good judges of a player's ability.

Lengthy runs in one or more of the Cup competitions kept

the turnstiles clicking away but a lot of money was spent on developing the Elland Road stadium, which must have affected the amount of money available for the Gaffer to spend on team strengthening. His first big-money signing in the top flight was Mick Jones, who became the first player to cost Leeds United a £100,000 transfer fee when he moved from Sheffield United in September 1967.

Mick earned the admiration of all who played with him because he was, first and foremost, a team player. He would run after the ball all day long if necessary. We loved him and as long as his name was on our teamsheet I was delighted. It wasn't often that I had to do it but if I had to hit a long ball upfield, I knew instinctively that he would be there waiting for it. He could do the lot. He was good in the air, quicker than people gave him credit for and he could hold the ball up and lay it off. He was also one of the most unselfish players I have ever seen. With a bit more self-belief, and a touch of Allan Clarke's arrogance, Mick would have scored more goals. He certainly knew where the penalty box was. You never had to shout at Mick Jones to get in the box. If Peter Lorimer or Eddie Gray or anyone else had the ball out wide, Mick would be there waiting. His eight goals in twenty-five league outings during that first season was not the tally expected, but once Allan Clarke – Revie's second big signing at a record £165,000 – arrived for the following season, it was a different story. They clicked and became the ideal attacking partnership. Mick was deadly when he came in at the far post with Clarke doing likewise at the near stick.

There were few I played against who were as good – Kevin Keegan and John Toshack at Liverpool, Ray Kennedy and John Radford at Arsenal are two pairings I can think of. Jones and

Clarke were an ideal foil for each other, Allan to sniff out the goals and Mick to do the battling and knock the ball down. Both were brilliant at what they did. Clarke was one of the best finishers I have ever seen with an instinct second to none and total and utter belief in himself. When he first came to Leeds United he would strut around as though he owned the place. The fee Leeds paid Leicester City for him was a British transfer record at the time and I think Allan loved that distinction. He got a bit carried away with himself at first but the rest of us were not going to let him get away with that. The Gaffer left the players to bring him down a peg or two and we sorted him out in different ways. He quickly became one of the lads. We were a close team, which was one of our biggest strengths. Talk to Allan now about Leeds United and the people he played with and he will rave about the club and those players.

Clarke had that competitive edge to his game and that arrogance all good goalscorers seem to have. Jimmy Greaves was the best player for scoring goals I ever played against and Denis Law was in that bracket, too. Allan was up there among the best but when people talk about great strikers of the past they don't mention Clarke in the same breath as Greaves and Law. When he was through one-on-one, nine times out of ten he would score. He was skilful, good on the ground, and at 6ft odd, also great in the air. Although he didn't have much meat on him, he was not afraid. It must have been a nightmare to play against Clarke and Jones. You had Mick, who wasn't all that tall but who had a great leap and would run all day, and Clarke who, given a sniff of goal, was deadly. Mick and Allan became big friends after they finished playing.

Peter Osgood was a striker I didn't like coming up against.

He scored one or two against me but Jimmy Greaves was the one I really hated playing against. At Tottenham one hot day at the start of a season, I was right on top of my game and hadn't given him a kick all afternoon. The ball was knocked down the middle late on and Alan Gilzean went after it. I was chasing and shouted to Gary Sprake to stay back but he took no notice, came out and clattered into both Gilzean and me. We all went sprawling, the ball went up in the air and who should be there? Yes, that's right. Greavsie just tapped the ball into the back of the net.

Revie used to tell us to forget about Greaves if he was outside the box because he wasn't the bravest of players or the hardest of workers but you had to start worrying if he was in the penalty area. Give him a sniff of the goal and, like all good strikers, he was fantastic. He didn't like it when the tackles were flying in but if you gave him a chance it was usually fatal. Jimmy used to pass the ball into the back of the net. He never really wellied it into the goal and he didn't score many with his head. When you think of the number of goals he scored, it speaks volumes for his skills on the deck. He was capable of brilliance and his goals-to-games ratio was exceptional. His record was 220 goals in 321 league appearances and in all domestic competitions for Spurs he netted 257 goals in 365 games. He was just as lethal for England, scoring 44 goals in 57 appearances. You can't argue with those figures – they are phenomenal.

Revie had a lot of trouble finding a centre-half to succeed Jack Charlton, who left Leeds in the summer of 1973 and became manager of Middlesbrough the following year. He tried Roy Ellam from Huddersfield Town and John Faulkner from Sutton United. John – or Max as we used to call him, after the golfer – had played centre-half for Sutton when we beat them 6–0 in an FA

Cup tie. It might have seemed surprising to sign a centre-half who had just played against you in a team so heavily beaten but Max wasn't a bad player. Brave and good in the air, he may have been a touch slow. Unfortunately for him, in his first senior game for us he suffered an horrendous injury when his kneecap was pushed a couple of inches up his leg. Roy Ellam had done well with Huddersfield Town but he didn't repeat it for us. I think the weight of expectations, following such an internationally renowned player as Jack, was too much and he couldn't cope with the pressure.

Tony Collins, our chief scout, had been looking all over Britain for a central defender. Revie began to push him hard to come up with the goods and Tony told him about a centre-half he'd seen with St Mirren.

'He's a gangly, nutter of a lad,' Tony explained, 'big and raw but he's got something and I think he has a chance of making it if he gets the right kind of coaching.' He was talking about Gordon McQueen.

The Gaffer was up for the gamble and we signed Gordon in late 1972 for £30,000. He turned out to be quite a player and went on to gain international honours with Scotland. His first game for us was against Derby County at the old Baseball Ground. The pitch was atrocious and near to the end of the match, shortly after Allan Clarke had scored to put us 3–2 up, Gordon headed a ball out of defence and went down with a bad attack of cramp in both legs. As I was running out I heard him call out, 'Don't leave me, Norman. Don't leave me.' He was in a lot of pain and obviously needed attention. Gordon had been playing part-time football with St Mirren and because he was such a big lad – 6ft 4ins and 13st – it took him a long time to come to terms with full-time training and to get fully fit. As a result, he tended to get cramp.

Gordon was first choice at the centre of our defence when we won the league championship in 1973–74. In the six years he played for Leeds, he made over 170 first-team appearances before being transferred to Manchester United for a then British record transfer fee of £500,000.

A year or so before Gordon joined Leeds, the Gaffer had signed Morton striker Joe Jordan, another young Scot, whom he had earmarked to take over from Mick Jones, and, not surprisingly, Joe and Gordon became great friends. Coincidentally, Joe, who cost Leeds £15,000, had been transferred to the Old Trafford club for a fee of £350,000 just a month before Gordon. Both were excellent signings for Leeds and after giving good service to the club their departures left Leeds with a profit of £800,000, which in those days was big money.

As time began to catch up with his side, Revie signed Trevor Cherry from Huddersfield Town for a fee of about £100,000. The beauty of this signing was that Trevor could play right-back, central defence or as a midfield anchorman, and he went on to give Leeds sterling service. He wasn't the biggest but he had a good spring so he could get up well and he was quick.

But at the start of the 1969–70 season the Leeds side was still very much made up of what you might call the Revie old guard and the desire for success was as great as ever. We were determined to carry on the search for further glory. With his demanding pre-season training schedules, Revie saw to it that we were a fit bunch of players but this was to turn out to be a season when even we could not quite cope with the excessive physical and mental demands we faced in a bid for three major honours. In a way, we fell victim to our own success. As the season built into a thrilling climax we just could not deal with the punishing schedule of matches we had to undertake. We made great progress in a bid to retain the league championship but had to accept the runners-up spot. We reached the FA Cup final and lost in a replay, and we got to the semi-finals of the European Cup. At one stage we had to play five games – four in the League and the first leg of the European Cup semi-final against Celtic – in just eight days. It was ludicrous. We went on to play nine matches in twenty-five days and all this after we had just completed three physically demanding FA Cup semi-final matches against Manchester United. The schedule ran like this: 28 March, Southampton (h); 30 March, Derby County (a); 1 April, Celtic (h); 2 April, West Ham (a); 4 April, Burnley (h). Then we had Chelsea on 11 April (at Wembley); 15 April, Celtic (a); 18 April, Manchester City (a) and 21 April, Ipswich Town (a).

A goalless draw at Hillsborough in that long drawn out FA Cup semi-final sent us to Villa Park for the replay where defences again dominated and the game ended 0–0. Three nights later we tried once more to settle the issue in front of a 56,000 crowd at Burnden Park, Bolton Wanderers' old ground. Billy Bremner did the trick for us by scoring the only goal of the game after about eight minutes, sending us to Wembley.

Those three attempts to overcome Manchester United's challenge took a great deal out of us but just two days after qualifying for the final we were back in league action at Elland Road kicking off that crazy eight-day period in which we had to play five games. Maybe it was a reaction to the second replay against the Reds but we suffered an embarrassing 3–1 defeat by Southampton. We were without a few players. I didn't play and

Billy Bremner, Mick Jones, Johnny Giles, Paul Reaney and Terry Cooper were also out but we still had a fair side. We actually took the lead through Peter Lorimer but the Saints won courtesy of two own goals, one from Jack Charlton, the other from Terry Yorath, and a penalty from Ron Davies after Terry Hibbitt had handled. Visiting teams feared Elland Road in those days and that defeat was our first home league reverse in almost two years.

Everton had been pushing us hard in the race for the league championship and our defeat by the Saints as good as ended our title bid. Everton went to the top of the table and I think the Gaffer felt our chance of another title had gone because for our next league game, at Derby two days later, he fielded a much-reduced side and Derby beat us 4–1. In fact, it was more like a reserve team but with a glut of fixtures coming up he felt it would be beneficial to give a lot of us some much-needed rest. We got no sympathy from the powers that be. They didn't consider the players and in their wisdom slapped a £5,000 fine on the club for fielding a weakened team!

There was just no let up. We didn't train – there wasn't really the time – and all the games seemed to roll into one. The adrenaline just didn't seemed to pump. Even for the FA Cup final we were, to a large extent, on autopilot. It was a very demanding time physically and mentally because there was so much at stake for us. These days the footballing authorities are more favourably disposed towards clubs who are hunting for success, especially in Europe. I think that makes sense, but it wasn't the case back in 1970.

Earlier our European Cup efforts had begun in record-breaking fashion as we beat SK Lyn Oslo 10–0 in the first leg of the first round at Elland Road. Mick Jones got a hat-trick, Billy Bremner, Allan Clarke and Johnny Giles bagged two each while Mike O'Grady got one. We put another six past them in the return leg in Oslo – not a bad way to mark your first tie in the European Cup. The Hungarian side Ferencvaros, who had provided such stern opposition when we edged them out in the final of the Fairs Cup in 1968, were our second-round opponents and we beat them 3–0 at Elland Road and 3–0 at their place – a pretty emphatic victory by any standards. The two quarter-final games against Belgian side Standard Liège were closely fought but we managed to beat them by the same score, 1–0, home and away to qualify for a Battle of Britain clash with Glasgow Celtic in the semi-finals.

We had been going great guns in the competition but we met our match in Celtic, who quite simply were too good for us. I'm not blowing my own trumpet here but, defensively, we had been in great form in the European Cup and we had reached the semi-finals without having conceded a single goal – and that was some record. So when George Connelly scored the game's only goal for Celtic in the first minute at Elland Road it was a big shock.

The game had aroused massive interest and it seemed that everyone wanted to see the second leg, particularly those living north of the border. Due to the huge demand for tickets the second leg was moved from Celtic Park to Hampden Park where, with a crowd of 136,505 – the biggest I played in front of – the atmosphere was electric. Billy Bremner shocked his fellow Scots after about quarter of an hour with an absolute cracker of a goal from twenty-five yards out. We were really up for the game and that strike by the wee man levelled the tie although I have to admit that, on the night, Celtic were in a different league. Jimmy Johnstone was simply great. He destroyed Terry Cooper with his speed and skills. With John Hughes up front, Bobby Lennox, Bertie Auld, Bobby Murdoch and Tommy Gemmell they had some terrific players. I played in a lot of European games for Leeds United but that Celtic side was probably the best I played against. They beat us 2–1, Hughes and Murdoch scoring their goals, to go through to the final on a 3–1 aggregate score. While Celtic looked ahead to a clash with Feyenoord in the final – which the Dutch side won 2–1 – we were left with the replay of the FA Cup final.

Four days before the Celtic disappointment we had played Chelsea at Wembley and we should have walked it – we would have done had we swapped goalkeepers. As it was, it ended in a draw – the first there had ever been in an FA Cup final at Wembley. Playing in a final, particularly the FA Cup, at Wembley with its lush green turf was always an exciting occasion, for players and fans alike. Unfortunately, for the 1970 final there was no lush green turf. The surface looked more like a beach than a football pitch. A hundred tons of sand had been spread over it in a bid to repair the damage that had been caused by staging the Horse of the Year Show there some little time earlier. It was dreadful. It was soft and it cut up something shocking but Eddie Gray made light of the conditions. His performance was outstanding and he gave Chelsea's David Webb a torrid time.

Jack Charlton gave us the lead after twenty minutes with a weakish header from Eddie Gray's in-swinging corner. Chelsea drew level just before half-time after Peter Houseman fastened on to a ball about twenty-five yards out. I could hear the fans shouting, 'Shoot, shoot,' and he took their advice. The shot didn't have all that much power in it and I wasn't too concerned until I saw Gary Sprake make a dive but instead of gathering the ball, he tried to scoop it up. It rolled under his body into the net. I couldn't understand what Gary was trying to do and neither could Jack. He was in familiar pose, standing over Gary and giving him a right ear bashing.

We managed to get our noses in front again when Mick Jones scored late on and we thought that would be it, but Ian Hutchinson grabbed the equaliser. Paul Madeley, who was playing at right-back in place of Paul Reaney, who had broken his leg in a league game, had taken the ball upfield. After beating one man, instead of staying on the flank he cut inside and was tackled. The ball broke and was knocked further upfield. Jack passed it back to Gary who tried to whack it away. Unfortunately, he bent it straight to one of their players. The problem was that we had not had time to move out and when the ball was quickly hit back in, Hutchinson got up to head the ball in from six yards. If Gary had picked it up, we could have got ourselves organised, but that was Gary. He was a brilliant keeper but prone to the odd gaffe. Don't get me wrong. All players make mistakes but when keepers make one it usually results in a goal.

Who can forget that headline-grabbing incident at Liverpool in the 1967–68 season when Gary threw the ball into his own net? It was a big laugh at the time but not for us or our supporters. Liverpool clearly thought it was hilarious. We, on the other hand, were dumbstruck. I was involved in what you might call the build-up to the goal, chasing after a ball with Roger Hunt in pursuit but there was no danger as I passed it back to Gary. He picked up the ball and I turned round and shouted for him to throw it to Terry Cooper, who was in the left-back position. As

Gary began to go through the motions of throwing it to Terry, Ian Callaghan charged across and closed Terry down. Gary checked his movement but in doing so, the ball came out of his hands and went into the back of the net. Behind him, the Anfield Kop went wild with delight. Jack Charlton was bemused.

'What's going on?' he asked. 'What's he done now?'

'He's thrown it into the back of the net, Jack,' I told him.

Jack shot across to referee Jim Finney and asked him what he was going to give.

'I'll have to give a goal, Jack,' was the referee's reply.

The incident came not long before half-time. They've a real wicked sense of humour in Liverpool and at half-time the strains of 'Careless Hands', a chart song sung by Des O'Connor, boomed out of the loudspeaker system. You could have heard a pin drop in our dressing room. It was like a morgue. No one said a word. After all, there's not a lot you can say to your goalkeeper after something like that. Looking back now, you have to laugh but it certainly wasn't funny to us at the time. We lost that game 2–0.

So the 1970 FA Cup final ended 2–2 after a game that, shall we say, was very keenly contested. I particularly remember one tackle by Ron 'Chopper' Harris on Eddie. 'Chopper' steamed in but the referee didn't book him or even award us a free kick. It was that sort of match. Only one player was booked in the whole of the game – Billy Bremner. A little while ago, a current referee watched a video of that game and did an analysis of it from a modern-day refereeing point of view. He said afterwards that had he been in charge that day under the instructions given to referees now, he would have sent four or five of us off and shown ten or eleven yellow cards. I've also watched the video and I have to confess that there were some horrendous tackles flying around.

In between the tackles, though, we played some good football. There is no chance of players these days getting away with some of the tackles and challenges that went on back in the sixties and seventies.

When we went into the replay against Chelsea on 29 April it was our last chance of salvaging something from a long and tiring campaign. The venue was Old Trafford and we were excellent in the first half but had only one goal to show for our efforts. Clarke went past two or three defenders before he knocked the ball to Jones, who went past another and hit a right-foot screamer of a shot to put us one up half an hour into the game. That's how it stayed until ten minutes from the end when Peter Osgood nipped in for the equaliser. I remember the build-up well. Paul Reaney was bellowing, 'Someone pick up Osgood, as he ran across with his man instead of staying in position and I have to admit that I didn't go with Ossie, who peeled off round the back. When the ball was knocked in, he scored with a diving header. That sent the replay to extra time and in the 104th minute Chelsea grabbed the winner when David Webb, of all people, got up well to nod in at the far post. After the time Eddie Gray gave him at Wembley I suppose Webb felt that he had more than got his own back on us.

It was another huge blow to our pride. Well it certainly was to mine. I'd had the stuffing knocked out of me. I was last off the field and I remember feeling absolutely gutted. We had been in with a good chance of pulling off a unique treble of the League, the FA Cup and the European Cup yet we had ended up empty handed. Fatigue and fixture congestion had cost us dear. It was heartbreaking. *You Get Nowt For Being Second* as the title of Billy Bremner's book so aptly put it.

11

REF TROUBLE, GIRL POWER, FA CUP DELIGHT AND DESPAIR

CELEBRATING a Cup success or a league championship win is a wonderful experience but, funnily enough, it is the shock defeats that stay with me. That may be due to professionalism but the hurt I felt when we were the victims of giant-killing acts also has a lot to do with it. People just don't let you forget those shock-horror defeats. Whenever I have a speaking engagement in the Sunderland area I'm taunted about Sunderland's FA Cup final victory over us at Wembley in 1973 and when I'm down Colchester way, people there won't let me forget the huge Cup embarrassment we suffered at Layer Road in February 1971.

Most teams suffer one or two games like that but they don't come any more embarrassing than our FA Cup fifth-round defeat at Colchester. At the time, they were in the Fourth Division and we were riding high in the First. The club had hired a private plane to fly us to Colchester. 'Billy Big Time' – that was us, travelling in style, as befitted one of Europe's leading clubs, as we were back then. These days most top clubs travel by air when faced with long trips in this country but back in the early seventies only a few clubs used that mode of transport for games in England. But what do they say? Pride comes before a fall? Well, it certainly did on this occasion. It was quite windy when we arrived at the Layer Road ground and walked out on to the pitch to have a look at it. It was the smallest ground in the League at that time and the Gaffer had worried about the tie ever since the draw was made. Jack Charlton was with me as we inspected the playing surface and I said to him, 'We're in for a hard time this afternoon, Jack.'

'Yes, Norm, I know it,' he replied.

We had a side packed with stars and international players yet we were two goals adrift by half-time and three goals down shortly after the break. Colchester had Ray Crawford who, at the age of thirty-four, was nearing the end of his career. He had won a couple of England caps when he was with Ipswich Town and, as we prepared for the kick-off, I sensed he relished the opportunity to play against a top club side and he marked the occasion by scoring twice against us. To make matters worse for me, I had been given the job of marking him. I hasten to add in my defence that there were mitigating circumstances. I was alongside him when the ball was whipped in from the flank but as I was about to make a challenge, Gary Sprake called out, 'Mine, Norm,' so I stopped. To my horror, Gary carried on, 'Yours, Norm,' but by then there was nothing I could do and the ball was in the back of our net. 'Sorry, Norm,' Gary called out as Colchester celebrated going one up after eighteen minutes. Crawford got the second goal about five minutes later when he beat Paul Reaney in the air and as Gary came out Crawford recovered well to prod the ball over the line. The third goal stemmed from a long punt down the middle. Reaney went after the ball but as it bounced Gary called out, 'Mine, Paul,' but Dave

Simmons clattered in and hit the ball into the back of the net. That was 3–0 to the underdogs after fifty-five minutes and, naturally, the home fans in the 16,000 crowd lapped it up.

I managed to pull a goal back with a header on the hour and I heard Crawford shout out, 'Look out, lads, they're just starting to play a bit.' Johnny Giles made it 3–2 and we had about another twenty minutes to fashion the equaliser but we couldn't get it. David had slain Goliath, as the press put it, and I think the whole country rejoiced. Colchester were superb and beat us fair and square to put us out of the FA Cup.

We were still going strong in the Fairs Cup. In fact, we reached the final, having beaten Liverpool in the semis on a 1–0 aggregate. Billy Bremner's goal in the Anfield leg of the tie proved decisive. Juventus were our opponents in the final and the first leg was in Turin. Although the Italians were favourites, we set off in good spirits with confidence high but we ran – sailed would be a more apt description – into troubled waters.

As it was a final, the Gaffer decided the wives and girlfriends of the players could go on the trip, but insisted they stay at a different hotel until after the game. But the best-laid plans can often go wrong and they certainly did on this occasion. Turin had been subjected to torrential rain before we arrived and as we were driven from the airport to the hotel we passed many fields that were virtually underwater. One of the locals told us that the city had been hit by a rainstorm every afternoon for the previous two weeks.

It was sunny during the day of the game but towards late afternoon the heavens opened and the rain teamed down. It was still coming down hard as we set off for the stadium and as we approached, we noticed lots of enterprising salesmen making a killing from selling plastic capes that were little more than dustbin liners, as people paid up in attempt to keep themselves dry. We thought there was no chance of the game going ahead. There were large pools of water on the surface of the pitch but, much to our surprise, the Dutch referee decided it was playable and that the game would go ahead. It really wasn't fit to play on but you could see the problem the referee had. This was a European final and some supporters had travelled a long way to get there. So we kicked off. The rain, however, kept on coming down and the conditions became farcical. We 'swam' our way to half-time after which the referee bowed to the inevitable and decided the game could not continue. The only course open to him was to abandon it which he did, but boy, did that decision throw up some problems. Fans had either to go back home on their charter flights and miss the re-staged game, or find extra cash and hotel accommodation to stay on for another two or three nights. The club managed to book our rooms for another couple of nights and also the rooms for our wives – but at their hotel, not ours. That was the problem.

It proved to be a bone of contention when the Gaffer said the wives would have to remain in their own hotel for another night or two instead of moving in with us as had been previously arranged. A couple of the wives, who shall remain nameless, didn't like this idea one little bit. They approached the Gaffer to register their protest and to ask him to change his mind. To make matters worse as far as the Gaffer was concerned, their husbands backed them up. The Gaffer went absolutely berserk. 'Right, that's it. Never again will the wives be allowed on any of our European trips,' he stormed. No sex, please, we're Leeds United, summed up that situation.

Some of the press boys who were on the trip with us picked up on the story but the rumour going the press rounds was that Revie had threatened to resign unless he got his own way over the issue with the wives. I never heard that one but it was the first time since we had all come together six years earlier that I had known any unrest among us. I did think at the time that it was a bit stupid of those concerned to do what they did. After all, we were there to play football. That was our job and we were there to try to win a European trophy. It certainly caused a ripple in otherwise calm waters.

Revie, of course, got his way. One or two of the wives flew back home but others stayed – at a different hotel until we played the game three nights later. Those fans who stayed on were rewarded by some thrilling football from both teams. Juventus had a very good side, with such players as Roberto Bettega, Fabio Capello, Pietro Anastasi, Franco Causio and the West German international Helmut Haller in their ranks, but we held our own and came away with a 2–2 draw. We went behind twice but came back each time, first through Paul Madeley and then Mick Bates. We drew 1–1 in the second leg and took the trophy by virtue of the away goals rule. It was our third Fairs Cup final appearance in five seasons and our second win.

In the League, we had to settle for runners-up spot for the second season in a row, as Arsenal pipped us for the title by one point. Towards the end of the season, when the battle for the title was reaching its climax, we were embroiled in a controversial game against West Bromwich Albion at Elland Road. A dreadful decision made by referee Ray Tinkler was at the heart of it, enraging Leeds fans, young and old. I have cause to remember that game perhaps more than anyone else because it was my pass that was intercepted by a player in an offside position. We badly needed to beat Albion to keep our championship challenge on course and, as you can imagine, the atmosphere at Elland Road was pretty tense. We had gone a goal down after sixteen minutes when Ally Brown scored but it was the second Albion goal that caused the problem. As Brown intercepted my pass, Colin Suggett was five yards offside and the linesman immediately raised his flag. For some reason known only to him, referee Tinkler waved play on, allowing Brown to have a clear run at our goal. As Gary Sprake ran out to challenge, Brown passed the ball forward to Jeff Astle who fired into an empty goal – but Astle was also in an offside position when Brown passed to him, so we were hit by a double whammy, you might say.

All hell broke loose. We were all incensed by the decision but although we managed to get the referee to speak to his linesman, Tinkler refused to change his original decision. The fans couldn't believe it and we suffered a pitch invasion. On they came, not just youngsters but grown men, and from the main West Stand too, all running on the pitch to protest. Later, a former referee, or someone who had connections with the FA, appeared on television and tried to make a case for the decision, saying that Tinkler was correct, but in those days when you were offside you were offside. There were no ifs or buts about it. And Suggett was offside. What maddened the fans more than anything was that the linesman had religiously flagged for everything all through the game and those decisions had been adhered to by the referee until this occasion twenty minutes or so from the end of the game. I read a quote from the then Lord Mayor of Leeds, an ex-referee himself, who was reported to have said he could find no defence for the referee.

Once the game restarted we managed to make it 2–1 when Allan Clarke pulled a goal back six minutes from time but we couldn't get another and we lost the game. Don Revie was furious at the referee's handling of the game and claimed that the goal decision had ruined eight and a half months of hard work. He also called for full-time referees to be appointed, a suggestion that generated numerous debates and was ridiculed in the media but another example of Revie being ahead of his time. Full-time referees operate in the Premiership now.

Tinkler's decision was a bad one and because of the trouble it caused, he never refereed at Elland Road again. Not only was it a bad decision it was a very costly one for us – it didn't just ruin our title chances for that season but for the next one as well. The FA decreed that, because of the pitch invasion, Leeds United would have to play their first four home games of the new season on away grounds. We didn't do too badly in those four games but we did drop points from two of them, which we rarely did at Elland Road in those days. We were pipped for the title by one point, so you can see my reasoning. Even now all these years later the name of Tinkler still sticks in my mind.

For the 1971–72 season the Inter Cities Fairs Cup was replaced by the UEFA Cup and we went out of the new competition at the first-round stage – something unheard of for us because we usually enjoyed a long run in Europe – when we lost to Belgian side Lierse SK, 4–2 on aggregate. We had won in Belgium 2–0 in the first leg without six of our international players but lost the return 4–0. Revie played several reserves because of injuries and rested Jack Charlton and me, although I came on for the second half when we were already 3–0 down. Young goalkeeper John Shaw made his first-team debut although Gary Sprake replaced him. Jimmy Mann, a young forward, also played, as did central defender John Faulkner and winger Chris Galvin.

To decide the final resting place of the old Fairs Cup, the powers that be arranged a play-off between the very first winners of the trophy and the last winners. Barcelona were the first to win it and we were the last so off we went to Spain to play a one-off game, which we lost 2–1. That was Joe Jordan's first full game for Leeds and he marked it by scoring his first goal for the club.

Coping with the Football Association's order to play our first four home games on neutral grounds caused a lot of problems from an organisational point of view. We played two of the games at Huddersfield Town's old Leeds Road ground, where we drew with Wolves and beat Crystal Palace. We drew with Tottenham at Hull City's Boothferry Park ground and walloped Newcastle United 5–1 at Hillsborough, the home, of course, of Sheffield Wednesday.

We went out of the League Cup at the third-round stage but it was by no means all gloom and doom. Revie had always adopted a cautious and very disciplined approach to our games, but now he took off the shackles and told us to go out and enjoy ourselves and give it all we'd got. He felt we were sufficiently experienced and skilful to know what to do if a game started to slip away from us. As a result, we went on to produce some of the best football we ever played.

In February we hammered Manchester United 5–1 at Elland Road as we chased the championship. The Reds had George Best, Bobby Charlton, Alex Stepney, Brian Kidd and Willie Morgan in their side but we hit top form and there was just no living with us that day. A crowd of over 45,000 saw Mick Jones grab a hat-trick and Clarke and Lorimer score our other goals. We didn't think we'd top that display but we did in our next home league game when we blitzed Southampton 7–0. Attack, attack, attack – that's what we did. We strung together pass after pass, especially against Southampton. The crowd were singing 'Ole' each time we strung passes together and I think at one stage we passed it about thirty times without a Southampton player being able to touch the ball. It was great stuff. We really enjoyed ourselves and it made a change to see headlines about Leeds United that read 'Super Leeds' rather than 'Dour Leeds'.

Needless to say, Jack Charlton and I had a very easy time at the heart of our defence. By the middle of the second half against the Saints we were fed up. It wasn't much fun standing around for long spells with nothing to do. It became too much for Jack and suddenly he shouted to me that he'd had enough. I said I'd had my fill of it, too, and I charged down the flank. To my great delight, Paul Madeley knocked the ball to me and in turn I crossed it to the far post. I hadn't any idea who was there but when I looked up there he was – Jack, grinning widely as he nodded the ball into the net. Come to think of it, he never thanked me for setting him up with the chance!

As a team we were really at our peak in the 1971–72 season. We had players all over the park who were capable of scoring goals and, of the regular players, only Paul Reaney and yours truly failed to get our names on the scoresheeet.

Sandwiched between our 5–1 beating of Manchester United and the 7–0 mauling of Southampton was a fourth-round FA Cup tie at Cardiff City, and on a heavily sanded pitch we turned in another excellent display, winning 2–0 with Johnny Giles getting both goals. We really wanted to add the FA Cup to our list of credits and were doing very nicely thank you. We had beaten Liverpool 2–0 in a second-round replay at Elland Road after having drawn 0–0 at Anfield, and eased past Bristol Rovers 4–1 in the third round. Our win at Cardiff earned us a fifth round meeting with Tottenham at Elland Road, which we won 2–1 to qualify for a semi-final against Birmingham City at Hillsborough.

Birmingham were in the Second Division but were making a bold bid for promotion – which they went on to achieve – and there was the usual hype that always accompanies a big match when a lower division club is up against a top club. Bob Latchford had been making noises about what he was going to do to Gary Sprake. He had written an article in a newspaper claiming that he was going to knock Sprake around and the Gaffer was a bit worried because Latchford had done it before. He didn't want Gary subjected to that sort of pressure so he made the surprise decision to bring in David Harvey. It was a big match for a goal-keeper to step into. David had been at the club for quite a while and played in the first team from time to time but he had never managed to make himself our first-choice keeper. Being pushed into such a big game didn't seem to bother him at all. He appeared confident enough but he didn't have much to deal with because we controlled the game from start to finish. Jack and I never gave Latchford a kick so David didn't have much of a problem in that respect. In fact, the game was an absolute doddle. We walked it and beat them 3–0 with two goals from Mick Jones and one from Peter Lorimer.

Arsenal were our opponents in the final but we went into it as favourites, and we had been tipped to win the league title as well. We had already lost two FA Cup finals – against Liverpool and Chelsea – and as we walked out at Wembley that thought was gnawing away at the back of my mind. It's great to get through to a final but it's terrible to lose. No one wants to know the losers and I didn't want a third disappointment. The game didn't provide the best of entertainment. It was a dour and hard-fought affair but we won it. Terry Cooper missed it after he broke his leg in a league game at Stoke City nine days before the final but Paul Madeley, who played in Terry's left-back position, was superb that day. As for me, well, I was really wound up for it. Charlie George with his long flowing hair was the darling of the Arsenal faithful and I was well and truly ready for him. I could not wait to get at him. As we walked out on to the pitch, I muttered to myself, 'This isn't going to be your day, pal. I'll make sure of that.' He did go close to scoring once when a ball dropped in our box and he hit it against the crossbar, but generally he didn't have much of a sniff. David Harvey handled the big-match occasion extremely well and pulled off some good saves, one of them a marvellous effort early on from an Alan Ball free kick.

Bob Wilson, Arsenal's first-choice keeper, was injured and didn't play in the final. Geoff Barnett took his place but you could not blame him for the goal we scored. Bob McNab should have tackled Mick Jones in the corner before the ball was crossed. He missed his tackle and Mick hit the ball into the middle where Allan Clarke met it with a wonderful header.

Mick got a terrible injury a couple of minutes from the end of the game. He fell and his arm bent the wrong way at the elbow. It makes me cringe even now when I think about it. As the rest of us danced about with joy at the sound of the final whistle, poor Mick was in absolute agony. We had been up to receive our medals when our medical man, Doc Adams, came over and asked me to help Mick up the steps to collect his medal from the Queen. Mick was in terrible pain. Every one of those famous old Wembley steps caused him great discomfort. He winced with the pain every step he took but he was determined not to miss out on collecting his medal from the Queen.

My mate Terry Cooper, his broken leg in plaster, raised his crutches in a victory salute as the tears streamed down his face when we paraded the FA Cup. It was a wonderful feeling trotting round Wembley with the Cup but all of a sudden the life seemed to drain out of me. This was something we had all wanted for such a long time. As a young kid back home in my native north east I had dreamt about doing a lap of honour at Wembley with the FA Cup but when we got back into the dressing room and I climbed into the bath, for some reason I can't explain, I felt deflated. I thought I might have been high on adrenaline but I wasn't. It was an anti-climax. I was completely drained mentally as well as physically. It was a strange feeling going from total elation to anti-climax at a stroke.

We had the usual after-match banquet in London but the players could not let their hair down or drink more than a celebratory toast because we had to leave the banquet early to travel to Wolverhampton in readiness for our final league game of the season – a key clash against Wolves on the Monday. Having to play such a vital game so soon after the FA Cup final was a ludicrous situation and one that I don't think would crop up now. Our hopes of a league championship and FA Cup double rested on the outcome but all our attempts to have the game played later in the week fell on deaf ears at the Football Association. Paul Madeley and I had been selected for the Home International match against Wales in Cardiff the following Saturday. Alf apparently insisted that the two of us should report with the England squad. There was little love lost between the two managers and I think this was Alf's way of getting back at the Gaffer, who had often found ways of keeping his players back from international matches in the past. Ironically, though, I had been one player who had always insisted – and had a battle or two with Revie in the process – on reporting for duty with England unless I was genuinely injured.

It was later suggested in some newspapers that there had been an attempt to persuade Wolves to lose that final game of the season. All I can say on that one is that I was there and I heard nothing and saw nothing to suggest that was the case. I don't believe it ever happened. A draw would have given us the title but we fluffed it and lost 2–1. Brian Clough and his Derby County side were already in foreign climes sunning themselves on an end-of-season holiday, having accepted they had finished in the runners-up spot. They couldn't believe it when news filtered through that they, and not Leeds, were the champions. It was another of those near misses we were becoming well known for but I don't put our failure down to that final match. We should have had it sewn up before then but we had suffered a couple of hiccups in the run-in, one of which was a 2–0 defeat at Derby at the beginning of April. We also lost at Newcastle but the big one was losing at Derby.

In 1972–73 we reached the FA Cup final again. I've mentioned the Cup defeat at Colchester being hard to stomach, but that was nothing to how I felt when we lost to Sunderland at Wembley. That defeat rankles with me more than any other. We had gone into the game as red-hot favourites. Sunderland were in the Second Division and not many people gave them a chance of beating us and lifting the Cup, but they played very well and proved everyone wrong. That was scant consolation to me. As a youngster I was a Newcastle United fan and as such I didn't like Sunderland. Also I never got on with Bob Stokoe, who was manager of Sunderland at the time, and I didn't like him either. So it really got to me when I saw him running on to the pitch to celebrate. Even now, whenever I go to speak at a dinner in the Sunderland area they bring up that Cup defeat. I usually get in first by announcing, 'All right, before we go any further, you deserved to beat us at Wembley in 1973.' That never fails to raise a cheer and it puts the audience in a good mood!

But on that day in May 1973, I felt total despair and disbelief at becoming the victim of another giant-killing act. Sunderland had done their homework on us. Dick Malone was at full-back and they had Bobby Kerr tucked in to stop Eddie Gray getting the ball. It worked well because they stifled Eddie. We never really got going until later in the game. Once Ian Porterfield had put Sunderland in front we started to play a bit. We nearly equalised but Jim Montgomery pulled off a brilliant double save, first from Trevor Cherry and then from Peter Lorimer. As soon as Peter hit it I was jumping up to celebrate because I thought it was certain to go in but somehow Jim managed to keep it out. I just couldn't believe it. Had that gone in I'm sure Sunderland would have been dead and we would have gone on to win, but it didn't and we lost.

Despite all the disappointments, Leeds United had a record most other teams would have been only too pleased to have. We were never out of the top four of the top division for eleven seasons – that's great consistency and quite an achievement for any team but we should have won more trophies than we did. I was in ten finals overall, which wasn't bad, but we won just four

– the FA Cup, the League Cup and two Fairs Cups – and that's not a good enough return. In addition, of course, I have two league championship winning medals in my trophy cabinet. But that defeat by Sunderland really was a bad moment and disappointments like that used to destroy me. Goodness knows what Revie used to think. There always seemed to be some major disappointment in a season and I would have loved to know just how much those set-backs hurt him. Yet he stuck by us and kept at it season after season.

We had gone strongly for a Cup double in 1972–73. Having won the FA Cup by beating Arsenal the previous season, we qualified for the now defunct European Cup-Winners' Cup competition and progressed to the final. We kicked off with a 1–1 first-leg draw over the Turkish side, Ankaragucu, and battled our way to a 1–0 home win against them in the second leg of the tie. The second round took us to East Germany for a game against Carl Zeiss Jena and that turned out to be quite a trip.

To enter East Germany we had to go through Checkpoint Charlie in the Berlin Wall, which divided east from west. We travelled from the airport in a luxury coach and had to stop in an area regarded as no man's land between the west side and the east. There we were subjected to the most rigorous of inspections and searches while armed guards looked on. We had to leave our coach and get on another for the drive into East Germany. This coach bore no resemblance to the one we had left behind. Actually, it seemed to be on its last legs. It was very old and it didn't appear too reliable to me. In fact, it looked as though it might fall apart. It had wooden seats and we had to endure a rough ride to our base in Jena. Just before we reached the hotel there was a loud bang and we lurched to a halt. One of the tyres had burst. I don't even know whether the coach was carrying a spare wheel or not because we didn't wait to find out. We walked the last half-mile or so to the hotel! After all that, we drew 0–0 and won the second leg 2–0.

We had an easier ride in the third round where we beat Rapid Bucharest on an 8–1 aggregate and then eased by Hajduk Split on a 1–0 aggregate in the semi-final. The final was a one-off game against AC Milan in Salonika.

A week or so before we set off for Greece, Sue and I had decided to have new carpets put down in our house but while we were in Salonika, there was a rumour doing the rounds that the Gaffer would be leaving to go to Everton. They wanted him and, to my surprise, he was actually thinking about going. The reason I know that is because the night before the game he came up to me and whispered, 'Norm, keep this between the two of us but if I go to Everton I'll be coming back for you.' I couldn't wait to get to the telephone to ring my wife.

'Sue,' I said, 'don't buy those carpets. We could be on the move!'

These things have a habit of leaking out to the press, however, and news of Revie's possible departure from Leeds came out because he had been spotted driving to Everton by some Liverpool fans. He stopped to ask them the way to the Everton chairman's house and they rang the newspapers. I still cannot understand why he didn't take the job. It was, apparently, a very tempting offer but, not for the first time, he stayed loyal to Leeds.

Other rumours going the rounds when we arrived in Salonika concerned the referee. Word was that we might have trouble with the match official and that, shall we say, he might look on Milan more favourably than on Leeds and would give us nothing. In the event, the referee denied us two clear-cut penalties and we lost 1–0. When someone comes up to you and says the ref is bent you don't believe it. We certainly didn't but perhaps we were naïve, assuming that UEFA appointed only the top officials. Although we dismissed the suggestions, by the end of the game we began to wonder. All right, we were a tough, uncompromising side but AC Milan kicked lumps out of us that night and were allowed to get away with it.

I remember Joe Jordan and Mick Jones being felled in the box, yet nothing was given, and one cross from Paul Reaney was blatantly handled in the penalty area and, again, the Italians got away with it. Milan had pulled most of their players back to defend after they took an early lead and the game became a nasty affair. I'm afraid this was one of the occasions when I was given my marching orders. As the final minutes ticked by I had become very frustrated. We were pushing strongly for an equaliser and as I ran forward with the ball, I was hacked down from behind. Gianni Rivera kicked me on the back of the calf and I lost my temper. I went after him and retaliated. A mêlée developed and someone's boot caught my ribs. When things cooled down a bit, the referee sent me off along with one of the Italian players, Sogliano.

At the end of the game the 45,000 crowd, made up predominantly of locals, stood and applauded us off the field and gave only muted acknowledgement to the Italian side, so they must have noticed something, too.

Some time later we found out that the referee had been suspended indefinitely. For us, though, it was another trophy we had been so near to winning and didn't.

12

TITLE KINGS, REVIE'S WALKOUT AND CLASHES WITH CLOUGH

W E DIDN'T know it at the time but the 1973–74 season was to be Don Revie's last as manager of Leeds United. He was to lower the curtain on a reign that had begun thirteen years earlier to take up the job of England manager.

He left Elland Road on a high because we bagged the league championship that season, holding off a strong challenge from our old adversaries, Liverpool, to win the title and qualify for another crack at the European Cup. Revie had longed for that opportunity to come his way again and I think he always felt that he would get the chance, so many people were surprised when he succumbed to the pressures from Lancaster Gate to take on the England job. I wasn't one of them. The chance of attempting to win the European Cup with Leeds would obviously have weighed on his mind but when you are asked to manage your country it is a great honour and one that you really cannot turn down. He had proved himself to be a very good manager at club level with Leeds and to me he was the ideal man to take over as England boss.

As for leaving Leeds, it would have been a big wrench but I sensed he had become concerned after our FA Cup final defeat by Sunderland. He wasn't quite as happy at Leeds as he had been. Although he hadn't shown it publicly, deep down he had been extremely upset by that result. I think he began to wonder if we might be past our sell-by date as a major force and it seriously crossed his mind to leave after that defeat. At the back of his mind, I think he knew there was bound to be a time when he would have to break up his 'family', even though he would have loved a second crack at the European Cup. Had he stayed at Leeds, I think we would have won it.

Our intention at the start of the 1973–74 campaign was to win the league championship. The Gaffer called us all to a team meeting just before the season began and told us, 'We're going to win the title and we're not going to lose a single game.' That was the plan and we set off at such a cracking pace that the players began to believe it wasn't an impossible mission to go through the league programme undefeated. We won our first seven league games, and in some style, too. Included in that 'Magnificent Seven' run were victories at Arsenal, Tottenham, Wolves and Southampton, and at home we disposed of Everton, Birmingham and Wolves again. We scored nineteen goals in those games and conceded four.

The game I remember most from that little lot was the one at White Hart Lane. We always seemed to play there at the beginning of a season when the weather was red hot. Inside the first couple of minutes, Peter Lorimer picked up a ball on the halfway line and slotted it through the middle towards Billy Bremner, who was lurking on the edge of the 18 yard box. As the ball went past him, Billy whacked it with his right foot and it flew into the bottom corner of the net. We were really buzzing after that one. Billy got a second a few minutes later and we scored a third shortly after that. Paul Reaney was involved down the line, Johnny Giles and Peter Lorimer carried on the move and when the ball was crossed to the far post Allan Clarke was there waiting for it. He had the time and space to control it, just like in a practice game, and he seemed to wait for ages before knocking it into the net. We were three up after less than half an hour against a side who were usually a major obstacle on their own ground, but they were great goals.

The first team to take a point off us were Manchester United, who came to Elland Road in our eighth game of the season and held us to a goalless draw. We set a record for the longest unbeaten run from the start of a season – twenty-nine games in all, of which we won nineteen. All good things come to an end sometime and our run was ended at Stoke City's Victoria Ground in our thirtieth game. They beat us 3–2 after we had gone two goals up. We opened the scoring with a cheeky goal after quarter of an hour when Billy Bremner, as alert as ever, took a free kick very quickly – too quickly for Stoke who were busy trying to organise their defence. The keeper didn't have a chance. We got another about five minutes later and we thought our unbeaten run was safe. We very rarely lost a two-goal lead. But Stoke hit back with a goal from full-back Mike Pejic and we went in at half-time all square after Alan Hudson grabbed Stoke's equaliser. The match was settled when Denis Smith got the winner, and I was left kicking myself because I had a great chance to make it 3–3 when the ball came to me on the edge of the Stoke six-yard box. Unfortunately, I headed wide. It was after this game that the Gaffer waved his chequebook about, threatening to sign new players unless we pulled our socks up. But even he couldn't get away from the fact that it had been a terrific run for us. The foundations had been laid for us to win the title for the second time in our history, although we stuttered a bit after that defeat at Stoke. We drew a couple of games, beat Manchester City at home but then lost three games on the bounce, away at Liverpool and West Ham and at home to Burnley, who walloped us 4–1. We lost just four games during the whole of the league campaign and ended on 62 points – five ahead of Liverpool.

Having set out our stall to win the title, we weren't too bothered when we went out of the League Cup at the first hurdle. We got to the fifth round of the FA Cup before losing to Bristol City in a replay. At Ashton Gate, Keith Fear equalised Billy Bremner's opener and we lost at Elland Road when Donny Gillies scored the winner by lobbing the ball over David Harvey. They were in the Second Division at the time and managed by Alan Dicks, who was later to take me to Bristol. One of their players, Gerry Gow, had a reputation for putting it about a bit and boy, did he kick lumps out of Billy Bremner and Johnny Giles. He was a tough little fella and he showed it in both games, but especially in the game at Ashton Gate. Jack Taylor was the referee for both matches and I thought that he let quite a bit go.

In the UEFA Cup we reached the third round where we lost to Portuguese side Vitoria Setubal. We won the first leg at Elland Road 1–0 on a bitterly cold December night but they went 3–0 up in the second leg before Gary Liddell pulled one back. It wasn't enough to stop them going through but, to be frank, we weren't all that bothered because we had our sights firmly set on the league championship.

When Revie chose to throw in his lot with England, the move

e 1973 European Cup-Winners' Cup final against AC Milan in Salonika, which we lost
), was a bad-tempered affair, not made any easier by some indifferent refereeing. I was sent
just before the end along with a Milan player. Here, though, one of the Milan players
ldn't wait until the end of the game to exchange shirts with me.

e Kop at Elland Road salute our 1973–74 championship-winning season.

Leeds chairman Manny Cussins presented me with this silver tray in 1973 to mark my 700th game for Leeds United.

Hobbling at Elland Road in November 1974 after having had a cartilage remov

Lowest point of my career – having dropped a clanger that led to Poland scoring and Engla failing to qualify for the 1974 World Cup finals, Bobby Moore and trainer Harold Shepherds try to console me as I leave the Wembley pitch.

Highest point of my career – being voted the first ever Player of the Year by the Professional Footballers' Association in 1974.

Left: Showman Duncan
McKenzie was one of
Brian Clough's signing
for Leeds in 1975.

Below: Brian Clough
didn't last all that long
Leeds but one of his fir
matches in charge was
FA Charity Shield mat
at Wembley against
Liverpool in August 19
Here he is on the bench
alongside Reds boss Bil
Shankly.

hard-man reputation resulted in fans creating a 'Norman Bites Yer Legs' banner that first
~eared in the mid 1960s. It was updated for our European Cup final against Bayern Munich
'aris in 1975.

~en received a 'Norman Bites Yer Legs' trophy from the Bradford branch of the Leeds
~ted Supporters Club and here I'm sharing a laugh about it with my son Michael (*left*) and
'riend Richard Kett.

Left: Oh yes it is! It's panto time in Leeds ba in 1975. Jimmy Armfie wrote his version of Cinderella and the Lee players put it on for th fans. I'm the wicked Baron Hunter while Bi Bremner played Butto and Duncan McKenzi complete with long blc wig, was Cinderella. Th show was so popular w had to stage it for a second night.

Below: Even at my fifti birthday bash we coulc resist the chance to tal bit of golf. Here I'm showing off a new clut former Leeds United backroom man Cyril Partridge (*left*), Mick Bates and Eddie Gray (*extreme right*).

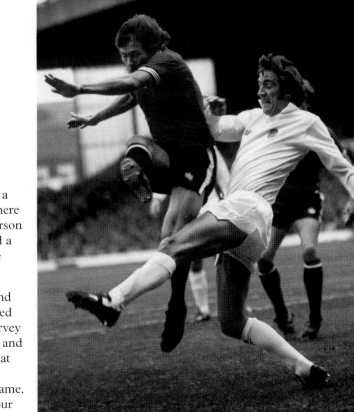

ht: I never shirked a
le in my life and here
I giving Stuart Pearson
Manchester United a
e of my aggressive
ending.

w: Baseball Ground
t-up – Leeds United
keeper David Harvey
arates Franny Lee and
I after we had a go at
i other during an
dent in a league game.
were both given our
ching orders.

Alan Dicks, Bristol City's manager, talked me into signing for the Ashton Gate club.

I loved my time at Bristol City. Here I'm moving forward with the ball being chased by Manchester City's Mick Channon.

turned out to be a nightmare for him. The reason I thought he was the ideal man for the job was that I knew how meticulous Sir Alf Ramsey had been and the attention he paid to detail and planning, and while Revie had a different personality, he managed in a similar way. Also, Les Cocker was with England and the two had a great working relationship when the pair of them were at Leeds, so it seemed an ideal partnership.

Revie won his first two or three games in charge of England and it appeared he was up and running. Then, for some reason, the wheels came off. The results got worse and one thing that really surprised me was when he made Gerry Francis captain. I thought he would have gone for a player with a northern club, who would have been a strong captain, but strangely he seemed to go the way the press wanted him to go. That had never happened before. He made his own decisions no matter how popular or unpopular they might have been. He was very strong in his management but with England he seemed to change and I think he tried to pacify the press with his selections. You are under greater media attention as England manager because everything you do is scrutinised nationwide.

Another mistake he made was to try to generate a club atmosphere on the international scene. It didn't work. He tried introducing carpet bowls and bingo but that approach just didn't catch on at that level. At Leeds, we had grown up with it and we enjoyed it. It threw up a load of banter and friendly rivalry. It kept us together and passed the time on what could have been tedious away trips. With England, Revie was dealing, in the main, with experienced international players. There wasn't, nor could there be, the kind of 'family' atmosphere he had fostered at club level. Carpet bowls and bingo didn't appeal to them as they had done to us when we first started out. I couldn't see Mick Channon, Peter Osgood and Rodney Marsh suddenly being up for that kind of thing.

I was delighted when Revie selected me for two or three games but after that he had a quiet word and told me it would be difficult for him to keep on picking me for the squad. Although I wasn't playing badly, he told me that other players and fans might think that my selection was down to favouritism. That was fair enough by me. If that is what he felt, so be it.

Sir Alf tended to stick by the same squad of players, introducing the odd one or two, but Revie brought in so many that he was accused at one time of cheapening the England cap. He never had a settled side and was not the success I thought he would be in the role. When he was in charge of Leeds, he was named Manager of the Year on three occasions, but he was unable to make the same sort of impact at international level. He lasted three years before leaving in controversial circumstances. I think he felt that he might get the sack, so he accepted a post with the United Arab Emirates. He had sold his story to a national newspaper and set out for the UAE in disguise. He told me later that he would definitely do things differently if he had his time to come again, by resigning first and then taking another job. He got a lot of criticism for doing it the way he did and I suppose he brought that on himself but it was sad for the man who had been such a great manager at club level. He remains Leeds' most successful manager. The club did not have much of a history until he took over.

Revie had built a great side at Leeds and brought the very best out of his players. I will always remain grateful to him for what he did for me. He made me a competitor and whenever

I went out on the pitch I gave everything, whether for Leeds or England.

As far as we were concerned, there was no such thing as a friendly, not in the sense that we have them today. All so-called friendly games were very competitive. You were playing for your country and you went out with the sole intention of giving your best, and you wanted to win. If you were substituted playing for England, you were absolutely devastated. That was the attitude every one of us had. There was none of this nonsense of making seven or eight substitutions at half-time. I was once substituted playing for England against Scotland and, believe me, I was gutted. I was playing against my clubmates, Joe Jordan, Peter Lorimer and, I think, Eddie Gray. Joe had destroyed me in the first half and Joe Mercer, who was England manager at the time, took me off at the break. Well, you didn't want that. You didn't throw the shirt away in disgust or anything like that but you took it as a personal insult.

I wasn't too happy, either, to see the Gaffer pack his bags and head out of Elland Road in the summer of 1974. He often said he would never fancy telling players to whom he was so attached and whom he had nurtured and turned into major players over the years that their time was up. I honestly couldn't understand that. He had done well for us and we all appreciated that. Professional footballers know when their time is up or when they are nearing the end of their careers and if he had come to me or Billy or Johnny and told us he could no longer select us for the side, I'm sure we would all have accepted it. In addition, Revie had signed some players who could carry on the success, such as Gordon McQueen to take over at centre-half and Joe Jordan to succeed Mick Jones, and he also had Mick Bates, Terry

Yorath and Trevor Cherry. Paul Madeley was still there so it would not have been that hard for the Gaffer to have split up his team and rebuilt. I really think he left because he dearly wanted the challenge of managing England.

To say I was upset when I found out the Leeds board had appointed Brian Clough as Revie's successor was a massive understatement. I just couldn't believe it. I found it absolutely amazing. He was the last person I hoped to see take over as Leeds boss. I really don't know what the board were thinking of in appointing a man who had been openly critical of the club and its players. Clough didn't like anything to do with Leeds United. At a major Sportsman-of-the-Year dinner when Peter Lorimer got the award, Clough was there to make the presentation but he kept everyone waiting while he went to the toilet. When he returned, he shocked everyone at the event by lambasting Peter. As you can imagine, there was no love lost between Revie and Clough and one of the first things Clough did when he moved in at Elland Road was to have the Gaffer's desk and chairs moved out of the manager's office.

When he got the job I thought straightaway, 'That's me out of the door.' Cloughie and I never got on. We never saw eye to eye with each other. He had been out of the dug-out to shout at me on a number of occasions during matches because he took exception to some of my tackles, so I felt my days at Leeds were numbered. He hadn't liked the way I played against his teams so he surely wouldn't want me playing for his team. I could only play it by ear.

The first morning, Jimmy Gordon, who had joined Leeds as part of Clough's backroom team, took training. As the time went on, there was still no sign of the new manager and we kept on asking Jimmy, 'Where is he?' There was no sign of Clough for five days. Then one morning he appeared and as we all gathered, it immediately became clear how hostile he was towards us.

'You lot who played under Revie and won all those caps and medals,' he said, 'well, find the biggest dustbin you can and chuck them all in there because you cheated to get them.'

Honest to God, as I looked round the room, I saw disbelief on the faces of the players. In his next breath, he said to Eddie Gray, 'You've been injured that much if you had been a racehorse you would have been shot by now.'

This was not the sort of thing to get you off on the right foot with a new squad of players. Good man management? Hardly. How can you talk to players like that and then in the next breath expect them to give everything for you? It just doesn't work that way, but that was Clough's way. He seemed hell bent on upsetting as many of us as he could as quickly as possible. If that was his aim, he succeeded. But it didn't end there. He had more in store for us.

One of our first games under his management was away at Stoke. He didn't select me for the team but I travelled with the squad. Don Revie always insisted on his players wearing suits and ties so that's how we were dressed. I can't remember what Clough was wearing but I think it might have been a tracksuit. The weather was poor when we arrived at the hotel. In fact, it was raining as we got off the coach. He stood there looking at us and as we automatically walked towards the hotel entrance he said, 'No, this way,' and walked us all the way round to the back of the hotel. Then he stood on the grass and talked to us for five or ten minutes about what he planned to do but he didn't tell us what the team would be. So, there we all were, standing around in suits and getting wetter and wetter. In all honesty, that's not the kind of thing you do to your players. That little stunt sowed more seeds of discontent among us. When we went inside and had our meal you can imagine what the mood was like. We were all chuntering on about how he had treated us.

The following day when we were boarding the coach for the drive to the ground, he was waiting again. As I got on the coach along with David Harvey, Clough announced to us that he would be bringing Peter Shilton to the club, and in his next breath he said he would also be signing Colin Todd. This was a manager telling two players who were just about to go out and play for him that he would be signing two new players who played in their roles. How's that for man management? He seemed deliberately to go out of his way to unsettle players. I remember him giving Giles and Bremner the biggest telling off I have ever heard any player receive. I cannot remember which game it was but it was at half-time. He verbally ripped them to shreds. It was unbelievable and the pair of them never said a word in response, which was unusual for both of them. Getting such a telling off was something new to them because Revie had never ripped into those two. He would sell his point to them but never in the way Clough did.

I admit I never liked Clough and I don't think he liked me, either. He certainly didn't endear himself to the vast majority of the Leeds players he inherited. In fact, almost to a man we could not believe how he came to be appointed manager in the first place. Our dislike of him was well documented in the press at the time and resulted in the chairman, Manny Cussins, calling for a meeting with us. We were happy about this but were amazed when Clough told us he wanted to sit in on the meeting as well.

We weren't having that and Johnny Giles told the chairman as much. The chairman agreed and we all had our say. Manny was there with another director and they asked for our opinions. The consensus was that Clough had to go. One player came right out and said he didn't think Clough was good enough to manage Leeds United. Usually the quiet type, we were surprised at how forceful he was. He made his feelings known in no uncertain manner. That was the effect Clough had on us.

No one defended him because of the things he had said about us and the way he had deliberately tried to make us feel uncomfortable. We left the chairman in no doubt as to what we wanted. Call it player power or what you like but we wanted the man out.

However, not all of us disliked him. Allan Clarke was pro-Clough – Clough liked Allan because he was a goalscorer, very much as Clough had been in his playing days – but he was in the minority.

We played seven games with Clough as manager and won just one. He was quite active in the transfer market during the short period he was at Elland Road, bringing in striker John O'Hare, who was a good player, midfield player John McGovern from Derby in a £125,000 deal and Nottingham Forest striker Duncan McKenzie for whom he paid £240,000. Johnny Giles or Billy Bremner were left out to make room for McGovern in midfield. I felt sorry for McGovern because trying to take over from either Billy or Johnny, who were such crowd favourites at Leeds and great players too, was an almost impossible task. He was on to a loser from the start and he had an absolute nightmare for the six months he was at Leeds. He and John O'Hare played only a handful of games for the club.

McKenzie was a character. I think Clough thought that Duncan was Scottish. He called Billy Bremner into his office and asked him what Duncan was like with Scotland – at least, that was the story that went the rounds at the time. I know Duncan very well now but at the time he joined Leeds, few of us had much of a clue about him. Duncan has the gift of the gab, which serves him so well in his current role as an after-dinner speaker, and he could certainly talk a lot when he first joined Leeds. He boasted that he could do this, that and the other. He set himself up a treat when he bragged that he could throw a golf ball the length of a football pitch and that he could jump over a Mini car – or we thought he had. Of course, we goaded him into proving his boasts. Being a bit of an all-round sportsman, I decided to take him on and so, too, did Mick Bates, who had played a bit of cricket. At the time, the ground was being re-developed at the Elland Road end. The famous old Scratching Shed had been dismantled in readiness for an up-to-date new stand. We went to the Kop end and I threw first, the ball landing just over the halfway line. Mick threw a little bit further than that and then it was Duncan's turn. He took a couple of strides and hurled the golf ball. It soared what seemed like a million miles into the air before it came down, bounced on the concrete at the Scratching Shed end and flew right over the stand. It was unbelievable.

After that, we had to test the Mini-car boast. One of the girls who worked in the office at Elland Road owned a Mini so we drove that into the West Stand car park. It was raining very heavily at the time. That didn't deter Duncan but one or two of the rest of us were having serious doubts about the wisdom of setting up such a challenge in what were very bad conditions.

Duncan was a top-priced player and here he was about to undertake a stunt that was potentially quite dangerous. One slip on the wet tarmac and he could have fallen and broken a leg – or suffered the type of injury that might even have finished his career. I have to confess that my 'bottle' had gone and I wished we had never taken it this far. Duncan wasn't a bit concerned. He simply took a run and jumped over the car. He did have to put one hand on the roof to make it but he'd proved his point again. The rest of us had to agree that he was as good as his word

It didn't take us long, however, to find out that he wasn't what you would call a team player. Teamwork had been our strength through the Revie era, we all played for each other, but Duncan was more of an individual. He was very skilful and I have to admit that he was a success wherever he went. He scored goals and was a big favourite with the fans and you couldn't knock that. He was an idol at Everton. Eddie Gray was just as skilful. He had as much if not more than Duncan in the skill department but Eddie knew the game. Like Duncan, he would take on two or three defenders and beat them but when it was the right time to pass the ball he would pass it. Duncan didn't do that so much.

I remember Duncan's first training session with us. I have good cause to because he made a fool of me! He had possession of the ball and as he approached me he called out, 'Nutmeg, Norman.' He teased me and, sure enough, knocked the ball through my legs with great ease. The rest of the lads fell about laughing because not many players did that to me. Duncan could play and although we viewed him with great suspicion when he first came, like the fans, we took to him after a while. I don't think anyone could help but like Duncan. He was a livewire in the dressing room, too, but he didn't stay at Leeds all that long. He was there for about two years and in that time he scored thirty goals in eighty appearances before he was transferred to the Belgian club Anderlecht. We played them in a pre-season tournament and I promised myself before the game that I wasn't going to let Duncan have a kick – and he didn't get one.

Clough's short but turbulent stay at Leeds attracted enormous publicity. The press were camped at Elland Road almost every day because they felt something was always likely to happen – and often it did. Taking everything into account, I think that Clough was just a bad choice for the Leeds job. You cannot deny what he achieved with Derby County and Nottingham Forest. He won European Cups and league titles. The only thing he didn't win was the FA Cup. His record was very good. He didn't have his trusted assistant Peter Taylor with him at Leeds. Taylor had been with him at Derby and Brighton and remained at Brighton when Clough moved to Leeds. Although Clough had Jimmy Gordon as his trainer, he virtually managed on his own at Leeds. The Clough-Taylor relationship resumed later when Clough moved on to Nottingham Forest.

Frankly, I don't think Clough could cope with having sixteen full internationals in the squad. I honestly don't think he knew how to handle us. His brief when he took over at Leeds was to break up the Revie side but he went about it in the wrong way. He came in like a bull in a china shop when he might have been much better advised to take things a little steadier. We all knew that, as a team, we could not go on forever. No team can and we had almost got to the point where changes needed to be made.

As things turned out, the axe fell on Clough before it fell on any of the players. He lasted forty-four days before he got the chop but he didn't do badly out of that very brief spell as Leeds boss. If you believe what the papers reported, he walked away with a sizeable tax-free sum of money and a Mercedes car. He said in his autobiography that the money he got from Leeds set him up financially and enabled him to manage exactly as he wanted to. He claimed he could do what he liked in management afterwards so that, at least, would be consolation for his unsuccessful efforts at Leeds.

While the two of us never hit it off, one of the most amazing stories relating to Clough concerned him and me at the time he was given the boot. On the night he left Elland Road, I was attending one of my testimonial meetings at the ground along with my committee chairman, Gabby Harris. Suddenly, there was a knock on the door and in walked Clough. He had a large bottle of champagne with him, which he duly handed to me. Then he turned to the guys who were on my committee and told them, 'You lot who are looking after this lad – work as hard as possible to earn him as much money as you can. There is no one else deserves it more than he does.' You could have knocked me down with a feather. Then he came up to me, took back the bottle of champagne and walked out. It was only after the meeting that we found out he had just been sacked. That was another side to Brian Clough, one that I had never seen before. When you think that he and I had never hit it off and that on occasions we had shouted at each other, it was quite extraordinary. Despite having just been sacked, he had taken the time and trouble to find out which room I was in and had come in to urge my committee to earn me as much cash as they could. I just found it amazing but Clough was nothing, if not, unpredictable.

Having experienced the managerial antics of Clough made me appreciate all the more the management style of Don Revie. He stood no nonsense, of course, and he was a hard taskmaster but he cared passionately about his players and their welfare and in return he had our full backing. We would have done anything for him.

13

END OF AN ERA, BRISTOL CITY AND A PAY-RISE SHOCK

FOLLOWING the board's U-turn on Brian Clough, news filtered down to the players that a quick appointment had been made and that Johnny Giles would become player-manager. Apparently, he had been interviewed and accepted the job. Everything was supposed to have been agreed and an announcement confirming the appointment was expected to be made to the press early the next morning. That announcement, however, was never made. Why? Well, apparently, Billy Bremner said he wanted the job and the board thought that if they appointed one of these two at the expense of the other, there could be some unrest in the dressing room.

The job eventually went to Jimmy Armfield, who had had some success in his first managerial role with Bolton Wanderers. We didn't mind. Anyone, we thought, was bound to be better than Brian Clough had been. So pipe-smoking Jimmy arrived and replaced the brashness and unpredictability that characterised Clough with calmness and indecision. Jimmy was a real nice guy and there was no doubt that with the great experience he had gained playing for Blackpool when they had a side that was greatly admired, and of course England, he had a wide knowledge of football. He was – and still is – well respected in the game but as far as Leeds United were concerned, he wasn't hard enough.

Jimmy was totally the opposite of Clough but he wasn't the strongest of managers, although he did break up the Revie team. He went about it in a much less obvious way than Clough had done, getting the job done gradually. Over the course of his management at Leeds, he got rid of me and offloaded Billy Bremner, Terry Cooper and Johnny Giles. Billy went to Hull City, Terry to Middlesbrough, Johnny to West Brom, and I went to Bristol City.

The press and the players came to regard Jimmy as being a little hesitant in his decision-making, which wasn't all that encouraging in view of the fact that we were playing in the European Cup. In fact, we did very well in that competition, reaching the final, but we were a team of very experienced players who knew the game inside out. We were in our tenth consecutive season in Europe. In addition, most of us knew it was our last real chance of winning a major European trophy, or any trophy for that matter, so we were definitely up for the challenge.

We didn't do all that well in the League, having to settle for ninth place – the first time in eleven seasons that we had finished outside the top four. We went out of the League Cup in humiliating circumstances, beaten 3–0 at Chester, who were then in the Fourth Division, and we were knocked out of the FA Cup after a marathon sixth-round tie against Ipswich Town. We played each other four times before Ipswich ran out 3–2 winners at Filbert Street, following draws at Portman Road, Elland Road and Selhurst Park.

However, we had our eyes firmly fixed on the European Cup and we kicked off the campaign shortly after Clough's departure. The confidence that had been so badly shattered under his management returned as we swept FC Zurich aside 4–1 in the first leg at Elland Road.

We lost the away leg 2–1 but had a comfortable enough aggregate margin to take us into the second round against our old European foes Ujpest Dozsa. We won 2–1 in Hungary and beat them 3–0 at home. Everything was going according to plan and by the time we disposed of Anderlecht in the third round on a 4–0 aggregate we were beginning to think we had a serious chance of making it to the final. It was during the home leg of this tie that Armfield took the decision to substitute Billy Bremner. He was the first manager to do that and Billy didn't like it one bit. We were 2–0 up with about a quarter of an hour still to go when Jimmy decided to make the substitution. Billy looked absolutely amazed when he was taken off. He really couldn't believe that he of all players was the one to go. It had never happened to him before in sixteen years, other than when he was injured.

'What, me?' he said to Terry Yorath, who was coming on as his replacement.

'Yes, it's you,' Terry replied.

I think Jimmy had decided to make a bit of a statement. He was attempting to get the message across that no longer were the old warhorses immune to change. Jimmy was showing that he wasn't afraid to become unpopular, but he played Billy in our next game, a league clash at Ipswich Town, which we drew 0–0, and he made a point of saying how impressive Billy had been in that game.

We were drawn against Barcelona in the semis. They were a great side, including Johan Cruyff and Johan Neeskens in their team. We had worked our socks off to get that far and I was really up for the game.

The first leg – our sixtieth match of that season – was at Elland Road and Armfield left me out. It was a bitter pill for me to swallow and I was gutted. I loved European nights at Elland Road but with Barcelona as our distinguished visitors, I had to be content with a place on the subs bench. You have to respect the manager's decision but it didn't mean that I agreed with it because I didn't. I had great experience and I thought I should have been in the side. A crowd of over 50,000 packed the stadium and the atmosphere was fantastic. Billy Bremner and Allan Clarke scored and we jetted out to Spain for the second leg with a 2–1 advantage, Juan Manuel Asensi having scored for Barca. I roomed with Johnny Giles and we were chatting about the game. We didn't know what the team would be but Johnny didn't think Peter Lorimer or I had much of a chance of playing. Imagine his reaction when the team was finally announced and both Peter and I were in while he was out! He was gobsmacked and stormed off to see Jimmy in his hotel room but it made no difference. No indecision there – just as there hadn't been when he left me out.

Welsh international Terry Yorath, who hadn't been among the regulars before Armfield arrived, played in both legs of the semis and the final. Jimmy quite liked Yorath but the problem for Terry was that the fans were always on his back. He could play superbly for eighty-five minutes and be man of the match but if he had a dodgy five minutes, the fans would slaughter him. Certain players seem to be singled out and it was just unfortunate for

Terry that he was one of them. I don't suppose he was thinking about that, though, as we ran out at the famous Nou Camp in front of 110,000 spectators. The atmosphere was simply electric. Peter Lorimer scored a great goal after the ball was flicked on by Joe Jordan. He hit it from an angle eighteen yards out and the ball flew into the net. Barca equalised before we suffered the blow of having Gordon McQueen sent off but we managed to hang on for a 1–1 draw, going though to the final on a 3–2 aggregate to meet Bayern Munich.

Gordon's dismissal meant that he would miss out on the final and the poor guy was in tears in our hotel after the game.

We hadn't been favourites to get the better of Barca but we proved everyone wrong. We could adapt very well to playing in Europe and we had come up with the goods. Now all we had to do to realise our big dream was beat Bayern Munich.

Having edged our way past Barcelona we were walking on air. We had reached the pinnacle of club football and it was such a great feeling. I couldn't wait for the final but I very nearly didn't make it. It was only thanks to the Boss's indecision that I eventually did play. On the Tuesday or Wednesday before the game we had a practice match. Everyone was standing around waiting for the teams to be announced and I was told, not by Jimmy, I was in the reserve side. Trevor Cherry would take my place alongside Paul Madeley in the first team.

After the practice game, Syd Owen came up to me and said, 'If he thinks you're not playing in this final, he's another think coming.'

When the day of the game came and our team was announced, I was in and Trevor Cherry was substitute. I think that showed Jimmy's indecision but if he had thought the right thing to do was leave me out all he needed to have done was tell me. All right, I would have been upset and annoyed but as a professional I would have had to accept it. Everyone has his own ideas and the manager lives or dies by his decisions.

The Gaffer, as all the lads continued to call Don Revie, was in the front row of the stand for the final. It had been his dream to steer us to a European Cup final victory and he wouldn't miss the match, even if he didn't have control over us any more. It was a great pity that we couldn't pull it off.

A few decisions went against us and I think we were unfortunate not to have won the game. Peter Lorimer hammered the ball into the Germans' net but the goal was disallowed because Billy Bremner had strayed into an offside position. Whether he was interfering with play was open to question. All the German players, Franz Beckenbauer to the fore, surrounded the referee and he consulted his linesman before ruling the goal out. Bayern scored twice to lift the trophy that we had so dearly wanted. It was a massive anti-climax and when I got my losers' medal I was distraught.

To make matters worse, as we came off the field there was trouble in the ground. A lot of fans rioted and that had repercussions for the club because we were later suspended from European football. As we left the stadium, I was walking towards the bus where our wives were waiting, to hand Sue my medal, when a policeman stopped me and pushed me. I was in a foul mood and swore at him. He reacted by drawing his baton back ready to clobber me but, luckily for me, another policeman had noticed my club tie and told him to hold back. As if losing the final wasn't bad enough, I might well have had a battering from a policeman as well.

After the disappointment of that defeat I knew that my future with Leeds United was in the balance. Trevor Cherry took my place for the start of the 1975–76 season and I was on the bench again for our second home game, against Liverpool. We were under a lot of pressure and I was itching to get on but Jimmy refused. I got up and walked off, which was interpreted by many as a walk-out – a protest aimed at the manager – but I actually went to the toilet! At least, that was my story. We lost the game 3–0. I was back in the side shortly after that and finished the season having made thirty-one appearances. I scored a goal, too, in a 2–2 draw at Birmingham. I was also sent off, together with Francis Lee, in a game against Derby County at the old Baseball Ground.

The referee had given a penalty when Franny went down in the box. I can honestly say that I never touched him. I turned to go with him but he just put one foot behind the other and went down. Later, we had a little punch-up. I hadn't been on the top of my game and I was unhappy because Franny had conned me. We were losing at the time and when a ball dropped between us we went for each other, grabbing shirts, and I said to myself, 'Watch out, Norman, he's going to stick one on you.' I wasn't having that so I got in first and smacked him one. I had never done that before in my life. I don't know why I did it but I did. A ring I was wearing split his lip. The referee sent us both on our way, of course, and as we were going off, he said something to me. I gave him a dose of the verbals with my answer, he started on me and then everyone joined in. The Football Association charged both of us later but I got off and he was done for bringing the game into disrepute.

However, the matter didn't end there. I'd had my testimonial and picked up £35,000 and he challenged me, on TV, to fight him in the street for it. He said he'd give me 3 to 1. Well, I didn't fancy that one little bit. I didn't mind mixing it on the field with him or anyone else. Off the field, it was another matter. Franny, though, was known for the odd dive or two in the penalty area and in one particular season when he was with Manchester City I think he got quite a lot of penalties. People write and talk about present-day players diving in a bid to win a penalty but Franny and Rodney Marsh were absolutely brilliant at it back in my day. They used to run straight at you with the ball, knock it past you and then go down.

Whenever I go back to Derby in my role as a radio summariser I am invariably greeted by the whole sorry incident being screened over and over again on the television in the pressroom and around the stadium. I find it quite embarrassing. Funnily enough, I was reminded of the incident when I was speaking at a dinner in Bristol. A huge fella came up to me and said, 'Hi Norman.' I looked at him and thought to myself, 'I know your face, pal, but I can't put a name to you.' It turned out to be Derek Nippard, the referee who had sent Franny and me off in that infamous game. Naturally, we discussed what had happened and I told him again that he'd got it all wrong. Franny dived to get the penalty but he still wouldn't have it. Let's face it, referees rarely admit they're wrong!

The whole event, which, as you can imagine, was really blown up by the press, didn't exactly endear me to our manager. I understood, though, that Armfield had to make changes at Leeds. Don Howe, a greatly experienced and highly respected coach who had coached Arsenal and managed West Bromwich Albion, became Jimmy's assistant and I think he had a big influence over who should be moved out and who should remain. At thirty-two, I was getting on a bit and I knew that my days as a top-class footballer were numbered but I loved Leeds and I didn't want to leave. I didn't know whether the Boss wanted me there or not and that is never a good situation for any player to be in. So I came up with an idea that I thought would benefit the club, the manager and myself, and I went to Jimmy's office to put it to him. I told him I didn't want to move away from Leeds and that if he would extend my contract by a couple of years and up my wages by a small amount, I would stay and play in the reserves.

'I'll keep myself fully fit and use my experience to help bring on some of the younger players, and when you need me for the first team, I'll be there ready and willing to step in,' I told him.

Jimmy was having none of it. Puffing on his pipe, which he usually did to give himself a bit of time to think before he answered, he said he couldn't do that.

'What you mean is that you don't want to do that, and if that's the case, then fair enough – sell me,' I said.

Most days after that I pestered him to try to find out what was happening. Eventually, I found out that only two clubs were interested in me, or so I was informed – Southampton and Bristol City. Come to think of it, he couldn't really have got me any further away from Elland Road. I confess I had no particular leaning towards either of them and I told Sue that I would go to the club whose manager treated me better and was straightest with me. That was Alan Dicks, so I ended up at Bristol City and it was one of the best decisions I ever made.

After saying yes to City it suddenly hit me that I had reached the end of an era, one that had been so rich in experience, enjoyment, success and, yes, heartache. I was about to leave Leeds United and they had been my one and only club. Obviously, it was big wrench but all good things come to an end and, as I didn't fit into Jimmy Armfield's future plans, the time was right for me to go.

One of the things that really upset me, though, was that no one from the board of directors said anything to me. There was no official thank you or handshake. It wouldn't have cost anything but it would have meant a lot to me. After being part of the Elland Road 'family' for so long I was now surplus to requirements and that was that. It wasn't the kind of treatment I expected from the club and it saddened me greatly. I was at Leeds for sixteen years and had given them everything. I made over 700 first-team appearances so I reckon I gave very good value for money. All right, you don't want fanfares or anything like that but there was only one person from Leeds United who shook my hand and wished me well for the future and that was Maurice Lindley, who had been assistant manager under Don Revie for many years. I'm sure it would have been different had Revie still been at the club. I'm not saying he wouldn't have got rid of me because he might well have done so, but at least I would have had some thanks. His attention to detail was so great.

It was only after I left Leeds that I realised I hadn't been as well paid there as I thought I had. In fact, it was something of an eye-opener when I joined City. I went there thinking that, having played for a top club for so long, I had been on top money but I found that, as far as our basic salary was concerned, we weren't very well paid at Leeds. Compared to the wages City were paying some of their players, I was one of the lowest paid! At Leeds, the money was still made up with bonuses. I actually earned better wages with City than I did with Leeds. I was on about £180 to £200 a week at Leeds and at Bristol I was paid £240 a week. It was quite a jump from what I was earning at Leeds – £10,400 a year to £12,500. I should have paid more attention to money than I did. I should have been more forceful but early in my career I wasn't too bothered over money. I wanted to be well paid, of course, but it wasn't a priority. It was only after I got married and found myself with a mortgage, kids and other financial commitments that the whole thing changed and suddenly money became a more important issue.

Going in to see Don Revie about a pay rise was not some-thing any of us looked forward to. We would talk among ourselves about how much we thought we should be paid. I remember discussing it with Terry Cooper, Paul Madeley and Mick Jones. That was all well and good and we felt full of confidence after-wards – a bit of group therapy, you might say – but somehow the confidence seemed to disappear once you found yourself in the Gaffer's office. All of a sudden, it was you and him. You would come out having got what he wanted you to have. You found your-self saying, 'Thanks very much, Gaffer,' and almost bowing as you backed out of his office! Later, when you sat down and thought about what you had agreed to, you probably found you had signed a contract for four or five years when you only wanted two!

Shortly after I became an England international I went in to see him and he obviously realised I was going to ask for a pay increase because he got in first, before I had a chance to state my case.

'Don't get carried away just because you're an international. I don't want you coming in here and demanding this, that and the other because you'll be disappointed. We don't pay those fancy wages they get in London. This is the north. This is Leeds,' he said. I accepted his reasoning because he wasn't a man you could argue with all that successfully.

I spent three and half years at Ashton Gate and I enjoyed every minute of it. When I joined them in October 1976, City, who had been promoted to the First Division the season before I joined them, were struggling to retain top-division status and I was looking forward to helping them stay up.

It wasn't a bit like being at Leeds United. On my first day I arrived early for training and bumped into Jimmy Mann, a striker who had been at Leeds as a junior but hadn't made it there. He walked in with his bag and said to another of the City players, Tom Ritchie, 'Tell Norman what we do with our kit.' I thought that was a silly thing to say but Tom replied, 'You bring it with you in the morning and you take it home with you afterwards and get your wife to wash it ready for the following day.' Well, I thought that was a wind-up. After years of having my kit washed by the laundry ladies at Leeds, I couldn't believe that you had to see to your kit yourself.

'You what . . . you're joking, aren't you?' I said. But it was no joke. I'd been spoilt rotten at Leeds. This was life at a smaller club. Being at Bristol City was a wonderful part of my career and I look back on it with great affection but I have to confess that I didn't do my own washing. We got someone to do it.

After being at Leeds for so long, where we were always under so much pressure and in the full glare of the spotlight, it was more relaxed at Bristol and, from a purely selfish point of view, I enjoyed being looked upon as a more skilful footballer than I had been at Leeds. With Leeds I was always told to win the ball and give it as quickly as possible to someone who could play a bit – Billy Bremner, Johnny Giles or Eddie Gray. At Ashton Gate, all of a sudden other players were giving the ball to me to play a bit. I quickly cottoned on and every time someone won the ball I called out 'Yes' and to my surprise they passed it to me. As a result, I found myself doing more on the ball. I passed it around a lot more than I had done at Leeds and, probably at times, I got carried away. I also had a great rapport with the crowd at Bristol.

Our fight for First Division survival went on for most of the season and when we travelled to Coventry City for our final game there was a real dogfight going on at the bottom end of the table. Half a dozen clubs, including us, and Coventry, were still fighting for their First Division lives. Jimmy Hill was manager of Coventry and Alan Dicks had been his assistant at one time. With such a lot resting on the result, it was obviously a very tense situation but it turned out to be the strangest game I ever played in.

First of all the kick-off was put back fifteen minutes and by the time we started, all the other matches had kicked off. We needed a draw to stay up and I think a draw was good enough for Coventry, too. They scored first and got a second through Tommy Hutchison. Gerry Gow bobbled one in the bottom corner for us before Donny Gillies levelled the scores at 2–2. With quarter of an hour still to go to the end of our match, word filtered round the ground that Sunderland had lost so they were down, provided we held on for a point. I am not kidding, Coventry had the ball in their half, then it was passed down to our half and we knocked it around a bit. No one wanted to take any risks and I said to the referee, 'You might as well blow your whistle for time now, pal, because neither side is going to score again!' He said he couldn't do that, of course, but it was the most bizarre situation I had ever experienced in football. When the final whistle did eventually blow, Terry Yorath, who had been playing for Coventry, jumped up and down with joy and relief.

Coventry and Bristol City finished with 35 points while Sunderland were relegated with 34. Stoke City went down with the same number of points and Tottenham finished bottom on 33. It was a close call but we had held on to our First Division status.

We did a little better in the 1977–78 season and managed to finish seventeenth – one place above the previous season – but our final points total of 35 was only 11 fewer than Leeds United, who finished in ninth place. We were a very good home side and that stood us in good stead. The following season we showed a greater improvement by finishing in thirteenth place, but that was the pinnacle for us. In 1979–80 things took a downward turn and there was a lot of speculation that Alan Dicks would get the sack and that I would be handed the job in his place. I did not really fancy becoming a manager at that stage and, as my contract was up, I moved back north. At Bristol, Alan Dicks was moved upstairs and Bobby Houghton took over for a couple of years. I don't think there was much, if any, money available to make team changes and I realised that whoever became manager would not want me there, which was why I'd decided to leave.

In 1979–80 City lost their top division status and were relegated again the following season. I have some very fond memories of my time there. I thought it was a very happy club and one that was great to play for. I have a soft spot for them and always look for their results.

When I left City, I went back to live in Leeds. I had been wise enough to keep my house there and I hadn't been back long when two of my old Leeds team-mates came to my rescue. Jack Charlton, who had left Middlesbrough and was then at Sheffield Wednesday, wanted me to play for him and so did Allan Clarke, who had become manager at Barnsley. I decided to join Allan at Oakwell. I went solely as a player but, if I'm honest with myself, I have to admit that I was knackered. I was nearing my thirty-sixth birthday and was suffering the ravages of time. I didn't do too badly and played about fifty games for them but I couldn't play at the centre of defence. Allan played me at left-back and sometimes in midfield in front of the back four. We had a lad called Ronnie Glavin who in three-and-a-half seasons scored over 100 goals, and we weren't a bad side at all.

My body had taken quite a hammering over the years and the knocks I was getting were taking longer and longer to recover from. I never had an operation until I was thirty-two and that was for a cartilage problem, but from then until I was thirty-seven I had two operations for Achilles tendons, another cartilage problem, another knee operation and a calf operation. The injuries were coming too often for my liking. I could have carried on playing because, really, I couldn't have got any slower! I could have stood around more and knocked the ball about but recovering from injuries was becoming more and more difficult for me. I think my body was trying to give me the message that it was time to call it a day. I knew it was and I decided to stop playing.

I'd had a good innings – a very good innings. Not many players played until thirty-seven so I reckon I was very lucky.

Meanwhile, a lot had happened at Leeds United. They had gone through a few managers. Jimmy Armfield lasted four years before getting the boot and Jock Stein, like Clough, was in the hot-seat for only forty-four days before leaving to take charge of the Scotland side. Jimmy Adamson came in for a two-year stint but he wasn't the answer for Leeds and in October 1980 he resigned and Leeds, having noted the impression he had made at Barnsley, turned to Allan Clarke. With Allan gone from Oakwell, I was asked to become player-manager. Jeff Buckle was the chairman and I told him I would have a go. Like an idiot, that's about all I said to the Barnsley board. You would have thought I had learnt my lesson about money when I was at Leeds but I obviously hadn't. I never asked about a bonus if we got promotion or anything like that. I simply got stuck into the job and, much to my surprise, everything I touched seemed to turn to gold. I couldn't do anything wrong.

It wasn't long before I stopped playing, but I had Trevor Aylott, who was a big lanky striker, and I knew that Ronnie Glavin would get me goals. I also had Mick McCarthy, Ian Evans, Phil Chambers and Joe Joyce. McCarthy, a central defender, was special, Evans was another good central defender and we just went from strength to strength. We had a simple policy. We defended well, played to our strengths and used Aylott's height to good advantage. We hit balls up to him and other players would join in. Glavin, for example, picked up all sorts of goals from knock-downs in the penalty area and the tactic served us very well. We were promoted to the Second Division and the following season we finished fourth. With a bit more luck, we might have gone up. Ironically, that was the season Leeds came down, having finished third from bottom.

One or two clubs were showing an interest in me because of Barnsley's promotion. Tony Collins, a former chief scout of Leeds United, told me West Bromwich Albion were looking for a manager and what did I think about going there. I didn't think I had enough experience to do that job and never bothered following it up. As things turned out, I was stupid. I should have given it a go. Anyway, I decided to stay at Barnsley and eventually things there began to slide. No matter how well we did, there was always an undertone of money or, to be more precise, the lack of it. The Second Division at that time was good for Yorkshire clubs. It included Huddersfield Town and Sheffield Wednesday and, as we were all pushing for promotion, we pulled in the fans for the good old-fashioned derby games. We had an average attendance of about 25,000 if my memory is correct. When we played Sheffield Wednesday at Hillsborough there was a crowd of 45,000. But the subject of money kept cropping up and eventually I had to sell Aylott, which was the last thing I wanted to do. I did my best to keep him at the club but the board wouldn't let me. I tried to bring players in but it became very difficult and, to be honest, some of my buys weren't the best. I ended up getting the sack but I don't hold anything against Barnsley. I enjoyed my time there and they were very businesslike when they did get rid of me. They sacked me on the Friday and by the following Tuesday they had paid me what I was due, so they did right by me.

They were, however, a bit miffed when I walked into another job with West Brom. They obviously felt that I'd had it all set up before I left, which was not true. When I got the bullet at Barnsley,

I had no other job arranged. Johnny Giles had taken over at the Hawthorns and when he heard I'd been sacked he asked me to join him as assistant on a part-time basis, with Nobby Stiles coaching the juniors. It ended up as a full-time job, which meant driving to West Bromwich most days, a journey that I came to dislike more and more. I wasn't there all that long and in the summer of 1985 I accepted the job of managing Rotherham United. My decision to go to Bristol City was one of the best I ever made – going to Rotherham was the worst.

I took over from George Kerr who had been in the job for just two years. I was also there for two years and, as far as I am concerned, it was an absolute disaster. Managing Rotherham was a real eye-opener for me. It was years since I had been involved at Third Division level. I hadn't even seen a Third Division game for a long time, so I hastily rang Tony Collins and I also spoke to Terry Cooper and a few others in a bid to get myself clued up. I thought I would be all right because Rotherham had just sold a player to Manchester City and another player had been transferred, so I thought there would be a few quid to spend in the transfer market. Sid Dennis, a scrap metal merchant, was chairman and he had coaches already there on the staff, but when I arrived I found to my amazement that they had just nine professionals. I did buy one or two players – Dean Henderson, Kevin Smith, a centre-half, a midfield player and a little lad by the name of Gareth Evans – but they were all sold on. The chairman and I never really got on. It was just one of those things. He wanted the people he knew at the club. Looking back now, the two years I spent there were the least enjoyable of my entire football career.

14

HONOURED BY FELLOW PROFESSIONALS, SACKED BY WILKINSON

AFTER the stability of a sixteen-year period with Leeds United, where life was comfortable and for the most part rosy, being given the sack was quite a jolt. Barnsley sacked me and so, too, did Rotherham and Howard Wilkinson was to add to those dismissals shortly after he took over from Billy Bremner as manager of Leeds United in October 1988.

I had been out of work for a couple of months following my departure from Rotherham before Billy asked me to join his coaching staff at Elland Road and, as Leeds are my club, I was absolutely delighted to do so. Although I enjoyed my time back at Leeds, matters, unfortunately, turned sour. Billy had done a great job getting the club to the semi-final of the FA Cup in 1987, where we lost to Coventry City, and we went within a whisker of being promoted to the First Division through the play-offs in the same season. John Sheridan put us ahead in the play-off final against Charlton Athletic but they hit back with two late goals to retain their top-flight status and leave us in the

Second Division. Having got so close to an appearance in the FA Cup final, as well as promotion, there was a feeling of anti-climax and in the 1987–88 season we finished in seventh place. When the following season kicked off, you could sense that the board were none too happy at the way things were going and in September Billy got the chop.

After six seasons in the Second Division the board were desperate for the club to regain top-division status and they pinned their hopes on Howard Wilkinson. I played against him once when I was a junior but, as a player, he hadn't pulled up any trees. He was more successful as a coach and manager and made a habit of getting clubs promoted. He had coached Notts County into the First Division and was in charge at Sheffield Wednesday when they went back to the top flight. Somehow, Leeds managed to prise him away from Hillsborough.

When Wilkinson first arrived, he called the coaches together and chatted about his plans for the club and what he was going to do. He asked me what I thought about various things. There was no talk about sackings or anything like that but the following day he called me into the office and promptly fired me. Why he couldn't have done it the day before I don't know. He explained that he didn't want any ex-Leeds players on his staff. 'So I'm letting you go,' he added. I replied that that was fair enough, but actually it riled me to think that the reason he was giving me the boot had nothing to do with my ability as a coach but was because I had enjoyed success as a player in the club's most successful era. He also decided that the pictures of the Revie players that adorned the walls at Elland Road should be taken down. Perhaps he thought too many people were living in the past and reflecting too much on former glories. Maybe he felt

Above: My most successful spell as a manager was at Barnsley and striker Trevor Aylott, seen here in action against Queens Park Rangers, was one of my key players, but I was forced to sell him in the end.

Right: Mick McCarthy was another member of my Barnsley side.

Below: In thoughtful mood as I watch my Barnsley team in action.

Pictured with fellow coach Nobby Stiles (*left*) during my time as assistant to West Brom manager Johnny Giles (*centre*).

I went on the Great British Tour for over 35s to Brazil in 1989, seen here with Peter Osgood (*left*) and Pele.

rge Graham, manager from 1996 to 1998, always had a smile on his face even though he
to steady the ship when Leeds United were in danger of relegation from the top flight.
ny Floyd Hasselbaink (*left*) and Alfie Haaland are also in a good mood.

Bowyer matured as a player under David O'Leary's
agement and was a big hit during Leeds United's
mpions League season. He played in our 3–0
rter-final first-leg win against Deportivo La Coruna.

David O'Leary, who took Leeds
United on to another level, shouting
instructions from the touchline.

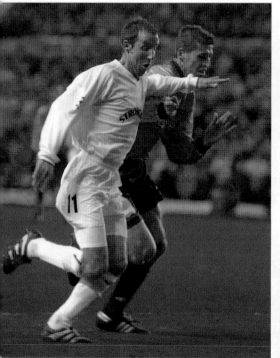

The turning point for Leeds United was the sale of Jonathan Woodgate to Newcastle Unite
The talented central defender – seen here challenging Ole Gunnar Solskjaer of Manchester
United – could have been a key figure in Leeds' fight to avoid the drop.

Terry Venables obviously didn't want to sell Woodgate and his body language suggests this
he sits alongside Peter Ridsdale at a press conference where the reasons behind the sale we
explained.

a nail-biting experience for Eddie Gray as he watches his Leeds United side lose 2–0 at
ne to Bolton in November 2003.

ds United's 4–1 home win over Wolves in February 2004 raised hopes that relegation just
ht be avoided. Here Alan Smith salutes his goal while Mark Viduka is also delighted.

What talent! The England and Scotland legends lunch in London in November 1999. *Left to right*: Jimmy Armfield, Terry Venables, Frank McLintock, Graeme Souness, Asa Hartford, Archie Gemmill, Andy Gray, Terry Butcher, Mick Channon and me.

ht: At Elland Road
ore one of my
adcasting stints
n BBC Radio Leeds.

ow: This is how it's
ne, son – taking on
ne of the children
n Lawnswood School
Leeds, where I helped
nch a new campaign
the Arthritis and
eumatism Council.

Here's one for the album – Sue surrounded by the family. *Left to right*: son Michael, baby Max (five months), daughter Claire, daughter-in-law Nicola and grandson Sam (two and a half years), enjoying sitting on Granddad!

the pictures were too daunting for his players whereas they should have served as an incentive and an inspiration to strive for similar achievement. He was looking to the future. That is what counted for him and while I could appreciate that point of view, I think there should always be a place for past achievements to be recognised.

During his time at Elland Road, former Leeds players were not welcome back at the club. You couldn't even get tickets for matches, unless, of course, you queued for them and paid. Other clubs would welcome back old players who had served them well in the past but, for a time, at Leeds the opposite was the case. Wilkinson didn't want anything to do with the old guard and if that was how he wanted to manage the club, fair enough. He was the boss and he would stand or fall by his decisions.

My next club was Bradford City, as assistant to Terry Yorath, but I was axed after just twelve months in the job. It was at that point I stood back and began to take stock of my life. I'd known nothing else but football and hadn't even considered a life outside it but now I felt I'd had enough. I'd stayed too long. I have to admit that I did one or two daft things once I had decided to leave football behind. I took a sports shop, then I had a stab at selling insurance – neither of which worked out for me – and I went into schools and did some coaching before taking up after-dinner speaking. Then I became a match summariser for Radio Leeds and this is the job I still do today. It's a job I really love. You don't have the pressures of coaching or managing a football club to contend with but you still have the chance to see the games and comment on them.

While I attempted to sort out my life outside football, Wilkinson made his mark at Elland Road. His job initially was to get Leeds back into the First Division and he set about it with great determination. In his first full season at the club he accomplished that task by winning the Second Division championship. The football Leeds played wasn't pretty to watch but it was a means to an end. With Wilko, it was a case of either you liked his style of play or you didn't. I have to confess that I wasn't keen on it but you cannot knock his record at Leeds. When he got into the First Division, he didn't play the long ball game. When you think about it, it would have been criminal to do so with Gary McAllister and the other creative players in midfield. He would have been daft to by-pass players of that calibre and he set the club on the right way again after eight years in the Second Division.

There is no doubt in my mind that Wilkinson pulled off a masterstroke when he persuaded Gordon Strachan to throw in his lot with Leeds, before they were promoted. Many people felt that Strachan, who was thirty-two and cost Leeds £300,000, was past it and that, after successful spells with Aberdeen and Manchester United, he would be content to wind down his career at Leeds. Not so – he proved to be a great buy. It was a lot of money for Leeds at the time and Wilkinson stuck his neck out to get him but the Scottish midfielder was an inspiration to the team. No one was more fully committed to the cause than he was. A fine player, all he had to do was keep himself fit and he did that remarkably well. In fact, you could say he was a fitness fanatic. Footballers should look after their bodies and it paid rich dividends for Strachan, who continued at Elland Road for nearly six years. In many respects, he had a similar effect on the side to Bobby Collins all those years earlier when Don Revie was making his mark. Good players always have time to control the ball and Strachan had that.

By this time I was well into my new career as a summariser of Leeds United games for Radio Leeds and we had a couple of spats with Wilkinson over what I had said on the radio about his team. I wasn't being vindictive, and people who know me and listen to me on the radio will know I don't criticise for the sake of it. I try to give an honest opinion of what I see and think. I will have a go if the team is not playing well but not in a nasty way. I like to feel that any criticism I make is constructive rather than destructive. Wilkinson obviously took exception to some of the things I'd said but he didn't challenge me personally. He called in the commentator, who at the time was Bryn Law, and gave him a rollocking. I told Bryn that if it happened again he wasn't to take any grief from Wilkinson.

'If he wants to have a go at me, let him do it to my face. I'll go and speak to him,' I said. I wouldn't have minded that but he just used to blank me. As a summariser, I would not be doing my job properly unless I said what I thought. Football is a game of opinions and everyone has one. You cannot say teams or players are playing well when they are not. I always try to give credit where it is due and I saluted Wilkinson's decision to bring in Eddie Gray as youth team coach.

The Leeds manager had changed his mind and turned to a Revie old boy – it was probably one of the best moves he made. The story goes that Wilkinson had been looking for quite a while for someone to take charge of the youngsters and almost everyone he turned to for advice about who they thought would be best suited for the job came up with the same name – Eddie Gray. Eddie did a great job in bringing on young players such as Alan Smith, Jonathan Woodgate, Paul Robinson, Harry Kewell, Stephen McPhail and Ian Harte, which was no surprise to those of us who knew him of old. We had long ago realised how good he was at coaching young players. However, Wilkinson didn't get the full benefit of Eddie's foresight and expertise because he was sacked before the young ones came through to the first team.

Whether you liked Howard Wilkinson's style of play or not, you had to admit that when he won the First Division championship in 1991–92 Leeds were a very good side. He had one of the best midfields around – Strachan, David Batty, McAllister and Gary Speed. They didn't come any better than that quartet.

Another excellent signing he made was Lee Chapman. Not the most gifted of players in the world, I'll grant you, but he was as brave as they come and he scored some great goals with his head. His touch let him down at times but his goal record speaks volumes. He came to Leeds midway through the promotion season and he provided the additional spark that was needed to clinch the Second Division championship by scoring 12 league goals in 21 outings, including the one at Bournemouth in the final game of the season that assured Leeds of the title. The following season, when Leeds were trying to establish themselves in the top flight – and finished fourth – Lee chipped in with a 21 league goal haul in 38 appearances. When Leeds won the First Division championship in 1991–92, he scored 16 times in 38 games. You can't argue with statistics like those. He had his critics but I wasn't one of them. I used to defend him to the hilt. In fact, I had one or two arguments over him with people who didn't rate him too highly.

Right-back Mel Sterland was another sound signing. Bearing in mind the strength and creativity of Leeds' midfield at that time, Mel's speed and crossing ability gave them a great option along the right. His crosses were food and drink to someone with the heading ability of Chapman. With Strachan also able to get forward and knock the crosses over, Leeds were always likely to be dangerous in attack.

Leeds won the First Division championship in their second season back in the top flight and that was a marvellous achievement for which Wilkinson deserves praise. He also had the guts to buy Eric Cantona, a big-name player whom he later sold to Manchester United after Cantona had allegedly demanded to be in the side every week. No manager can guarantee any player that and, if those were the circumstances, I would have sold him, too, had I been manager. To me, Cantona always looked as though he could be disruptive.

It was not so much Wilkinson's decision to sell Cantona that brought the criticism but the relatively small amount of cash – £1.1 million I think it was – he got for him. I would have wanted a lot more than that. At that fee, it was more like giving the player away. That, for me, was the start of the slippery slope for Wilkinson. Cantona went to a huge club, of course, and Alex Ferguson certainly got the best out of the player.

Wilkinson also stuck his neck out to bring Tony Yeboah, the Ghanaian international striker, to Elland Road. He was a similar type of forward to Jimmy Floyd Hasselbaink but few people had heard much about him. He scored some tremendous goals for the club, including a fantastic hat-trick in a European game against Monaco in Monte Carlo. He also scored a wonder goal in a hat-trick against Wimbledon, at Selhurst Park, and won the Goal of the Season award with another strike, this time against Liverpool. After Wilkinson's departure and George Graham's arrival he was transferred to Hamburg.

Wilkinson was at Leeds longer than I thought he would be –

eight seasons – and his overall record wasn't that bad although some of his later buys weren't that good. I'm thinking in particular of Tomas Brolin, the Swedish international who cost the club a lot of money – £4.5 million, according to reports at the time – and hardly played a game. His fitness was called into question at times and, with hindsight, his signing seemed ill advised. Matters came to a head at Wembley in March 1996 when Leeds played a disastrous League Cup final against Aston Villa, losing 3–0. It seemed an ideal occasion to play Brolin but Wilkinson turned instead to teenager Andy Gray, the son of former Leeds star Frankie Gray, and although Andy played well, Leeds, as a team, were not at the races. They were badly beaten and the Leeds fans, who had been solid in their support of Wilkinson, turned on him quite savagely. 'Sergeant Wilko's Barmy Army', as the fans delighted in calling themselves, vented their feelings as he walked off the Wembley pitch. His achievements in getting the club out of the Second Division and then winning the First Division championship had evaporated in the huge disappointment at that League Cup final failure. They booed him all the way off the pitch and I had never seen anything quite like that at Wembley. Deep down, I think he must have realised that that was the beginning of the end for him at Leeds.

Wilkinson was good at building teams but I think he found it difficult to buy and control established players. His problem was that he didn't improve on the championship-winning team. From being champions one season, his team struggled and plummeted next term to seventeenth place. We did have a better season in 1993–94 and 1994–95, finishing fifth on both occasions, but in 1995–96 we were back down to thirteenth. A poor start to the following season didn't go down well. A draw at Derby in the opening game of the campaign was followed by a home defeat by Sheffield Wednesday. A narrow home win against Wimbledon lifted spirits and a 1–0 win at Blackburn left us with a respectable seven points from a possible twelve. But the manager's fate was sealed after arch-rivals Manchester United walloped us 4–0 at Elland Road. It was the last straw for the Leeds board and the axe fell.

The manager's departure didn't come as much of a shock. There's no doubt he had enjoyed success at Leeds but things had turned sour for him and when that happens to a manager it is usually followed by the sack. It's a fact of footballing life that you have to take the bad times as well as the good ones. One of my worst moments in the game came in the 1973 season when I was playing in a key World Cup qualifying game against Poland at Wembley. I made a real hash of a tackle and Poland went away and scored. We needed to beat them to qualify for the World Cup finals. We went into the game having beaten Austria 7–0 but we managed only a draw against Poland and that wasn't good enough. That was the first time England had failed to qualify since we first entered the competition in 1950. For quite a while after that, wherever I played I was taunted by the fans chanting, 'Hunter lost the World Cup.'

To make matters worse, I had messed up my big chance. Alf Ramsey had left out Bobby Moore for the game against Austria and again for the clash with Poland. Paul Madeley was in the side and there was a chance, too, for central defender Roy McFarland. Emlyn Hughes was in at left-back and Tony Currie in midfield. The press had said that the Poland side were not up to much and it was one of the most one-sided games I had ever played in at international level. We went in at half-time goalless but Alf just told us to carry on playing and we'd win it. There was nothing more certain, he said.

Allan Clarke fired us into the lead and we thought we were on the way to victory but then it all went pear-shaped for me. This guy came across and I remember thinking the race for the ball would be a fifty fifty situation but he slowed up. I had set myself for the tackle, thinking he would keep on coming. Unfortunately, the ball went under my foot and he was off and away while I chased back, praying he wouldn't score. I thought Peter Shilton was going to save his shot – in fact, I thought at the time that he could have thrown his cap on it – but he didn't save it. I was distraught and I just wished the ground could have opened up and swallowed me there and then.

The first person to come up to me after the game was Bobby Moore. He put his arm round me to console me but I couldn't be consoled. Like an idiot, I said publicly that it was my fault. With the benefit of hindsight, I shouldn't have done that. No one else said a word – not Shilton, not anyone – and then I received dogs' abuse everywhere I went. Poland had beaten us 2–0 in Poland when Bobby Moore made a mistake without getting the blame that was heaped on me. Even so, we should have beaten the Poles at Wembley. We were the better side on the night. They kicked balls off the line and we had shots rebound off their bodies while on other occasions their goalkeeper Tomaszewski who, incidentally, had been described by Brian Clough as a clown, turned in a brilliant display.

England have been drawn against Poland quite a few times since then and that wretched incident seems to be shown on television over and over again. It's something I would really rather forget.

While that was one of the lowest points of my career, my greatest personal triumph was winning the Players' Player of the Year award in 1974. I really could not believe it when I was told I had become the first-ever recipient of that award. Don Revie knew that I had won it before I went to London for the dinner. It was supposed to be a secret to be revealed on the night so I don't know how he had found out, but he said to me before I left, 'You've won it, you know. So get that speech ready.' In those days, I hated having to make a speech so in some respects being told I'd won it made me feel worse. After the votes had been counted, we were told, it had come down to a contest between Ian Callaghan and me and everyone thought that Ian, being a gentleman and a good player for Liverpool, would get it. I thought so, too. Even though the Gaffer had told me I'd clinched it, I wasn't prepared to believe it until the announcement was made at the dinner. As I went up to collect the award, one of the guys organising the event whispered in my ear, 'We're running late so keep your speech short.' Fantastic, I thought to myself. I spoke for a couple of minutes and that not only pleased the organiser, it delighted me. Peter Barnes hadn't been able to say a word. He just froze. I was wearing a fancy yellow shirt with frills on it and took a bit of stick from some of the lads but it was one of the best moments of my whole career, a complete surprise but a wonderful one. That award is something I cherish to this day. To have been voted Player of the Year by my peers is something very special to me. There were a lot of great players around at that time and to have beaten them to it meant such a lot.

Actually, it makes a great Trivial Pursuit question. Who was the first player ever to win the PFA Player of the Year award?

Not many people get that one right! Naturally, the trophy, which is quite a large one, had pride of place in my house. I put it in a prominent position in the hall but over the years things get moved about a bit. It's not on show now but that hasn't diminished the pride I felt, and still do, at having been the first player to win such a prestigious award. When I do interviews at home, it's the one trophy they all want to see and that's when Margaret, the lady who comes to help Sue with the house, goes potty because she has to shine it up and make it sparkle.

There wasn't too much sparkle on the pitch when George Graham took over as manager from Wilkinson but I didn't have an issue with that. Leeds had been leaking goals left, right and centre and the one thing that was needed at the time was to tighten up in defence. From the outset, I believed Graham's appointment to be a good one. He had a no-nonsense approach to management at Arsenal where he ran a tight ship and enjoyed a lot of success. His sides were always difficult to score against and when he came to Leeds his first job had to be to tighten up the leaky defence, which he did. Mind you, we weren't too good to watch. We probably bored the pants off a lot of spectators. As one wag said to me, 'If Leeds were playing Wimbledon in my back garden, I'd draw the bloody curtains on!' But George did what was needed and the team began to pick up points and climb the table. George always had a smile on his face and he didn't bother over what people thought of him or his teams, woeful to watch or not. He just got on with his job and managed the club as he saw fit, and it worked. He made Leeds very hard to beat.

Another thing he did was to welcome back former players to Elland Road. In total contrast to Wilkinson, George thought it was a good thing to have us around the place, and would always acknowledge you. When he saw me, he would come over for a chat.

Leeds finished in eleventh place that season, having scored just 15 goals in home league games and 13 in away matches. The fact that they conceded just 13 goals at home – fewer than any other team in the Premiership apart from Aston Villa who conceded the same number – was a measure of their defensive strength. When you consider that Leeds had already conceded six of those goals before George took over, you get an idea of the defensive qualities he instilled into the team.

Having retained top-flight status in his first season in charge, George took the team on to another level in the 1997–98 campaign. Leeds clinched a place in Europe by finishing fifth behind Arsenal, Manchester United, Liverpool and Chelsea, and they did it in some style, doubling the number of goals scored. By this time, George had signed Jimmy Floyd Hasselbaink for £2 million from Portuguese side Boavista. I have to confess that I had never heard of him and I don't think many of the fans had, either. He didn't run around too much but he could score goals and he got better and stronger while he was at Leeds. Although he didn't get many goals with his head, he scored an awful lot of good goals from outside the box and his value soared. When he left in August 1999, he cost Atletico Madrid £12 million, which earned Leeds a massive profit.

It had been something of a surprise to many – myself included – when George agreed to take over at Leeds and while he did a good job for us, I always felt that eventually he would go back to London. After taking Leeds back into Europe, he didn't hang around to enjoy the fruits of his labours, preferring instead to become manager of Tottenham. He took some stick for leaving but I didn't blame him for grasping the opportunity. The way football is set up these days, I don't think you can blame anyone for doing what he thinks is best for him. The kind of loyalty that was in evidence when I was a player isn't there any more, whether it be players or managers. People used to stay at clubs for ten to twelve years but not many people are there that long now.

George was living in an apartment in Harrogate on his own and it can get very lonely. He once said that it was great when a match was on or when you were at the training ground but when you go home to an empty flat it's not much fun. I know that from personal experience at Bristol when I spent almost nine months living in hotels. I hated it. People think you're having a ball but whoever you are and wherever you go, you need your family there with you. If you're on your own and not happy off the field, it can affect your ability to do your job. So I wasn't surprised when George took the Tottenham job.

I honestly don't think he got enough credit for the job he did at Leeds. His side is remembered as boring, which it was at first, but people have always loved to criticise Leeds. Under George, it was only more or less what Leeds had come to expect down the years, and he was experienced enough to take it all in his stride. I thought he did a great job to get the club back on its feet again. He was very thorough in his approach and I think he had a bit of Don Revie in him as far as that part of his management went. He concentrated a lot on set-plays while under Revie we didn't train that much. The Gaffer did it more in team talks, speaking about opponents rather than showing people what to do.

George was responsible for bringing David O'Leary on to the coaching staff at Elland Road and that proved to be a good appointment for the former Arsenal defender because in a relatively short time he went from being a player to becoming a coach and to managing Leeds United, without any real experience. That was one in the eye for those who insist you should start at the bottom with a small club, learn your trade and work your way up.

15

LIVING WITH EUROPE'S ÉLITE AND RIDSDALE'S DEPARTURE

PETER RIDSDALE became chairman during the time George Graham was at Leeds and when everything went wrong four or five years later, I was reminded of something the wife of a friend of mine said to me after his appointment.

'Norman,' she said, 'I don't want a supporter as chairman of my football club. I want a businessman, someone who will run the club in a businesslike manner. I want someone in charge who will look after the pennies.'

I have to admit that I told her not to worry and that it was good to have someone at the top who was passionate about football in general and Leeds United in particular. I pointed out that the club was doing well and that the future looked as encouraging as it had done for a long time. But her words have flooded back to me on numerous occasions since the financial situation at Elland Road spiralled out of control. Unfortunately, her fears have been realised.

Ironically, if Ridsdale had had his way at the outset, David O'Leary would not have become manager of Leeds United.

Martin O'Neill, who was then at Leicester City, was widely accepted as being the number one choice to succeed Graham at Elland Road. That never materialised, however, and O'Neill stayed with Leicester although, of course, he later left there and went to Celtic. Once O'Neill had finally decided he wasn't coming to Leeds, it was only to be expected that O'Leary's name would be linked with the vacancy but when it was, he played a very astute game. He publicly claimed he didn't want the job and although he was put in temporary charge of the team, other names continued to be linked with the vacancy. In the end, Ridsdale turned to O'Leary.

The fans played a part in getting him the job because of the great reception they gave him at the UEFA Cup game against Maritimo in Madeira, even though the match itself was one of the worst games of football I have ever seen in my life. So while it was a gamble to put faith in an untried manager, it was a popular one with the supporters. Eddie Gray joined him as assistant manager and Leeds started to win games.

O'Leary got rid of many of the players George had brought in and gave the youngsters a chance to show what they could do. George had talked a lot about how good some of the young players at Elland Road were but he never put them into the first team. O'Leary did with great success.

On a personal level, he hardly ever spoke to me. It didn't start out like that. Soon after he arrived he invited me into the office. 'Come in, Norman, say hello to Eddie and have a cup of tea,' he said. We had a good chat and everything seemed fine but from that day forward David never spoke to me again in all the time he was manager at the club. That was his prerogative, of course. I believe he took exception to what some ex-footballers might be saying in the media but what did he do after he was sacked by Leeds United? Like a lot of us, he turned to the media and appeared on BBC television as a pundit.

It's undeniable that David O'Leary took Leeds United on to a new level. He brought the good times back to the club and no one wallowed in the glory of that more than I did. Leeds took the Champions League by storm and played some superb football. His side was entertaining and a joy to watch. Leeds became almost everyone's favourite other team. We were arguably the most exciting team in the country and television commentator Martin Tyler told me that he couldn't get enough of Leeds on Sky TV. They were good days and it was a real pleasure to be a Leeds fan. We walked tall and lapped it up. Whether he intended to or not, O'Leary changed the image of the club for the better with the entertaining way he played the game. He adopted an attacking style and Leeds scored plenty of goals. Whatever he did seemed to turn out right and his dealings in the transfer market in the early stages of his management were excellent. His team showed a good blend of top players with experience and young players who came in and performed brilliantly.

Lee Bowyer, who joined during the Howard Wilkinson era, used to run around like a headless chicken when he first played for Leeds. He didn't seem to know where he was playing or what he was doing but in O'Leary's team, he came of age as a footballer. I rated him an excellent player and how he performed to such a high standard during the many months of his court case I'll never know. He scored goals in the Premiership and in Europe and it was no surprise that he won the club's Player of the Year award.

Jonathan Woodgate's reaction to the court case, which he was also involved in, was quite the opposite to that of Bowyer. It obviously got to him. His whole demeanour showed he was worried about it. He lost weight and his play suffered. Before that, he had impressed me with his defensive performances and he looked as though he might be a top-class player in the making. His partnership with Rio Ferdinand at the centre of the Leeds defence had a good chance of becoming one of the best in Europe.

Ian Harte's prowess at dead-ball situations had people comparing him to David Beckham, and you could understand why. At one stage, Harte was so successful that whenever he stepped up to take a free kick you felt you could say to the opposition goalkeeper, 'Pick that one out of your net, son.' He really did knock in some magnificent free kicks.

Alan Smith, Harry Kewell, Michael Bridges, Mark Viduka, Stephen McPhail and Olivier Dacourt all came into O'Leary's side, so it was hardly surprising that Leeds were a force to be reckoned with. The glory days were back and that was absolutely magical for me. The atmosphere and passion generated by European nights at Elland Road were still just awesome as far as I was concerned. I loved them as a player and I looked forward to them just as much as a spectator. From the stand I watched Real Madrid, Barcelona, AC Milan, Lazio, Roma, Anderlecht, Valencia – they all came and it was wonderful to see so many great players. Watching Real Madrid, I got the feeling that they could move down field and score a goal any time they liked. If we'd scored one, they would have scored again. Some games were truly fantastic and the beauty of it all was that O'Leary's side held their own against the best.

George Graham's efforts in getting the club into the UEFA Cup in 1998 were admirable. We scraped through against

Maritimo after a penalty shoot-out. George left three days later and O'Leary was caretaker manager for the next round, against Roma, who triumphed on a 1–0 aggregate.

A second season in the UEFA Cup was much more encouraging and enjoyable. Leeds really showed their mettle and proved they were capable of competing with the best. Partizan Belgrade were beaten 3–1 away and 1–0 at Elland Road – which was more convincing than when I played against them back in 1967 when we beat them 3–2 on aggregate in the Fairs Cup. Next up was Lokomotiv Moscow. Having beaten them 4–1 at Elland Road, Leeds completed the job in style in Moscow, winning 3–0. Spartak Moscow, whom we eventually played in Bulgaria because of very bad weather in Moscow, were more of a problem but we got through on the away goals rule after a 2–2 aggregate scoreline to set up a tie with Roma. We got our own back on the Italians for the defeat they inflicted on us the previous season by beating them 1–0 on aggregate. Harry Kewell scored the only goal of the tie. A 4–2 aggregate win over Slavia Prague sent us into a semi-final tie against Galatasaray.

Spirits were naturally sky high at having reached the semi-finals, but in Istanbul the situation turned into a nightmare following the fatal stabbings of two Leeds fans, Christopher Loftus and Kevin Speight, on the eve of the first-leg game. I wasn't there but the news of the deaths of those two supporters left me feeling numb. I know there can be trouble before games when rival fans meet up, and that in itself is sad, but no one should lose their life following the sport they love. It was tragic. In the outpouring of grief that followed, supporters, not just from Leeds but from many other clubs too, sent floral tributes to Elland Road.

Peter Ridsdale handled the situation with great dignity and displayed a most caring attitude. Nothing was too much trouble for him. I don't think any other Premiership chairman could have dealt with it as well as he did.

The deaths of those two Leeds supporters put the game of football into perspective but the players were faced with having to go out and play a match – a semi-final at that – just twenty-four hours later and in a very intimidating atmosphere. When I was a player, we went to one or two places that were a little daunting. On one occasion, quite early in our European missions, we visited Naples, having won the first leg at Elland Road 2–0 when Jack Charlton scored twice. In the tough return, Napoli won 2–0. We had to flip a disc to see which side was to go through to the next round and we won the toss. We'd had a few problems when we ran out on to the pitch but as our coach drove out of the stadium after the game, it was pelted by missiles. We had to get down on the floor of the coach for protection.

Galatasaray are something else, though. Their fans don't possess the best of reputations with their 'Welcome to Hell' banners. Having to play after what had happened the night before and in such an intimidating atmosphere could not have been easy. I'm sure most of the players would have been thinking that they should not be playing out of respect for the two people who had died. There was a suggestion that the game be called off but, with a European match, there is the problem of people who have made their travel arrangements. Whatever the pros and cons of the situation, the Leeds side obviously didn't have the heart for the game and Galatasaray took full advantage to open up a two-goal first-leg lead.

The whole sad episode knocked the stuffing out of the team and they lost their next game, a league visit to Aston Villa, 1–0 and were then hammered 4–0 at home by Arsenal. That was not the sort of build-up required for the return meeting with the Turkish side. In addition, the funerals of the two fans took place during the week leading up to the second game. The possibility that trouble might flare at the game was also a worry but, as things turned out, it went off without any major incidents. Eirik Bakke scored twice for us, the match ended 2–2 and Galatasaray went through to the final on a 4–2 aggregate.

By finishing fourth in the Premiership, Leeds had done well enough to qualify for the 2000–01 Champions League. It was a great feeling being in Europe's most prestigious club competition for the first time – I could hardly wait for the campaign to start. I was well past my sell-by date as a player, of course, but the next best thing for me was to follow the fortunes of Leeds in my role as a football summariser for radio.

We had a tricky preliminary round to get through first but we managed to get past TSV Munich 1860 with a 3–1 aggregate win. We were now in the Champions League proper. I was walking on cloud nine, so what must the players have felt like?

When the draw was made we found ourselves up against Barcelona, Besiktas and AC Milan. The press, not very originally, labelled it the Group of Death and David O'Leary's Champions League novices were given little chance of advancing. The opening group game did little to suggest otherwise as we went to the famous Nou Camp stadium where Barcelona thumped us 4–0. Rivaldo opened the scoring after only nine minutes, Frank De Boer made it 2–0 on twenty minutes and Patrick Kluivert rounded off a sad night for Leeds with a couple of goals in the late stages of the match. The critics were quick to point out that the defeat underlined what they had thought about Leeds' ability to survive among the élite of European football. The players looked shattered and disillusioned after that experience but the defeat served as a warning of what to expect. They heeded the lesson and surprised us all with their ability to progress from such a tough group.

Six days after that drubbing, AC Milan came to Elland Road and, while we all hoped for the best, I suspect that many of us viewed the challenge O'Leary's young guns were facing with more than a little trepidation. We needn't have, though, because on a rain-soaked night Leeds pulled off a great result, beating the Italians 1–0. Lee Bowyer's long-range shot a couple of minutes from the end went in after goalkeeper Dida made a real hash of his attempt to save. Maybe there was a bit of luck attached to that win but it was a win and that seemed to instil confidence into the Leeds side. Our Champions League adventure was well and truly under way.

Six goals were put past the Turkish side Besiktas in our next game at Elland Road and that was followed by a goalless draw in Turkey. The big test was to follow when Barcelona came to Elland Road. We were seconds away from what would have been a great victory when Rivaldo grabbed an equaliser in the fourth minute of time added on. It was tough on the goalkeeper, young Paul Robinson, who had come into the side and done a fantastic job. However, we ensured our entry into the next group stage by drawing 1–1 with Milan in the San Siro. Milan qualified as group leaders with Leeds second. Third-placed Barcelona dropped into the UEFA Cup. We had survived one so-called Group of Death but went straight into another when the draw gave us Real Madrid, Lazio and the Belgian club Anderlecht as opponents. Great stuff! O'Leary's team had become so confident that the grouping held no fears for them. They were riding high, holding their own with the best and enjoying the experience. So was I. Leeds looked a good side and their achievements were hailed not just by their own supporters but by many others up and down the country. There was a real feel-good factor about Elland Road and we wallowed in it with no thought at all, of course, of what disasters might befall the club in the future.

When Real Madrid arrived it was fabulous to see world-class performers taking on Leeds at Elland Road. Back in my playing days we had a tremendous respect for Real Madrid's achievements and we had changed our playing strip to all-white in a bid to emulate the great Spanish club. Sadly, the Revie side never got the chance to play Real Madrid in European competition. Our paths never crossed. Now the opportunity was here but, unfortunately, Real Madrid won 2–0 with goals from Hierro and Raul. It was a memorable night all the same.

Another memorable night followed when we beat Lazio 1–0 in the Olympic Stadium in Rome. Alan Smith, who, along with the other young players in whom O'Leary had put his faith, was growing up fast as a player, scored the goal. After that, Anderlecht were disposed of 2–1 at Elland Road. We had a great result in the away game against the Belgian side, winning 4–1 with a superb performance. People were talking about Leeds as being the most exciting team in the country – and I think, at the time, they were. Next stop was at the famous Bernabeu stadium for the return with Real Madrid. Leeds lost 3–2 but were unlucky. A 3–3 draw at home to Lazio put us through to the quarter-finals. Considering it was Leeds' first crack at the Champions League, it was quite an outstanding achievement to get that far.

An inspired performance against Deportivo La Coruna at Elland Road enabled Leeds to take a 3–0 lead into the second leg in Spain but Deportivo were a very talented and well-organised side and they almost pulled the game round in the second leg. Leeds hung on and I was mightily relieved for us to come out of the game with just a 2–0 defeat. We met our match in the semis, though, when Valencia beat us 3–0 on aggregate.

The adventure was over but what a wonderful experience it had been for everyone concerned with the club. I thought O'Leary's management style had been excellent and that he had played the situation extremely cleverly. We all tasted the European scene and revelled in the atmosphere of it. When you look back at the football Leeds played and the results they were getting, it must have been a joy for O'Leary's players to report for training.

One thing I could not understand, however, was the decision to bring in Brian Kidd as first-team coach and put him ahead of Eddie Gray. It was something of a personal thing for me because of my friendship with Eddie but, even allowing for that, I found it difficult to accept. At the time of the change, Leeds were flying along as a team so why try to fix something that wasn't broken? Kidd might well have had different ideas from Eddie but as soon as he was appointed my thoughts were that Kidd would never be accepted by the Leeds fans purely and simply because of his previous connections with Manchester United. And he wasn't really accepted. Never once did I hear the Leeds fans chant his name.

On a personal level, travelling into Europe as a radio summariser was a very different experience from travelling as a player. In the Don Revie era, we were kept on a very tight rein whenever we went abroad. As a result, we saw very little of the cities we visited. This time, though, I could wander around and take in the sights, have a meal and a few drinks and get a 'feel' for the places. I also got a better 'feel' for the stadiums and how they operated on match days, especially for the media. The majority of the clubs were very well organised for the press. The press facilities, I thought, were generally better than they are at English grounds

Sadly, the Champions League adventure was not to be repeated the next season, 2001–02. Failure by one point to grab fourth place in the Premiership let Liverpool in and we had to be satisfied with another campaign in the UEFA Cup. It was a big blow, of course, but I didn't realise – nor, I suspect, did the fans – just how costly that one-point failure was going to be. The UEFA Cup is an important competition, and good to be involved in, but it doesn't bring in the millions that the Champions League does. It was a turning point for the club.

To perform at the highest level you need top-class players and Leeds had spent a lot of money bringing players in. O'Leary spent something like £90 million and that's a huge amount by any standards. He pulled in about £30 million from selling players and, after he was sacked, the club sold on some of the players he had bought. Caught up in the euphoria of it all, I was certainly not a dissenting voice when Leeds were shelling out millions. I didn't hear any caution coming from supporters, either. We gave the club credit for doing what they did. It's easier to talk with the benefit of hindsight but how many people warned, 'Don't buy this player or that player?' Nobody did. We all chased the dream – just as Peter Ridsdale did. Being a supporter, I was urging, 'Go on, let's go for it. Buy these players,' like all the others, because I thought we genuinely had a chance of continuing at the highest level.

As I have said, I thought David O'Leary bought well, especially in the early days of his management, but he must have felt he had a great chairman. When you consider the amount of money that was made available to him it added up to Ridsdale having total faith in his manager. David must have felt he could do no wrong and that he was at the best club with the best chairman – not to mention the good wages and good players. Everything he asked for, he seemed to get. Money was no object. O'Leary, as he often said, was young and naïve as a manager but whatever he did seemed to pay off. The way things were panning out for the club, he must have wondered whether management really could be as easy as it seemed.

Looking back now, I wonder whether O'Leary demanded too much of the board or if the board were too eager to sanction his spending. The conclusion I've come to is that it was a combination of both. The huge amount of money he was given to spend is usually entrusted to managers with a great deal more experience, such as those at Manchester United, Arsenal, Liverpool and Chelsea. He may have been a bit young in managerial terms to spend money to that extent but then the board seemed too easily swayed to agree. It was not an easy situation because had the board not granted O'Leary his spending powers, they would probably have been accused of lacking ambition and failing to back their manager. At the same time, having spent heavily, the board should have been in a position to know just how much in debt the club were.

The vast majority of the signings O'Leary made proved to be

good for the club but I would take issue with two of the later ones – Robbie Fowler and Robbie Keane, who were priced at a total of £23 million. Had I been manager, I wouldn't have bought them, not so much for the transfer fees that were asked, but more because I didn't think we needed them. I would have bought someone who could play wide right. At that time we had Lee Bowyer and Olivier Dacourt in midfield, we had Eirik Bakke to come in and we also bought Seth Johnson. Up front we had Harry Kewell, Alan Smith, Mark Viduka and Michael Bridges. As far as I was concerned, we could have done without Keane and Fowler, although Keane is a good player. Fowler was good in his heyday but from what I had seen of him on television, I didn't feel he was all that fit. The amount of money these two players cost was far too much and, taking into account their wages, it didn't add up to the best of business.

Many people criticised the £7 million signing of Seth Johnson from Derby County but I could understand the reasoning and went along with it. When he played for Derby against Leeds at Elland Road he was head and shoulders the best player on the park. I thought O'Leary had it in mind that Johnson could eventually take over in midfield from David Batty. Unfortunately, it didn't quite work out that way. Johnson struggled and, what with some injuries that affected his development, he did not have the impact I thought he would. It was a big disappointment.

When Ridsdale agreed to pay £18 million to sign Rio Ferdinand from West Ham, I just couldn't believe it. That was an astronomical figure. I thought, 'Well, we must have the cash to splash about otherwise you wouldn't do it, would you?' As we discovered later, there wasn't sufficient cash to support the ambitions of the club. Ferdinand, however, improved greatly as a player while he was at Leeds and a lot of the credit for that is due to O'Leary who, of course, had been a centre-half himself in his playing days.

Apart from missing out on the Champions League, the court case involving Jonathan Woodgate and Lee Bowyer was another major body blow. In my view, the publicity surrounding it did untold damage to the club and I don't think we ever really recovered from it. The book that David O'Leary wrote entitled *Leeds United on Trial* added to the problems. I think he was very badly advised over that. The club's dirty linen was washed in public and the club was hung out to dry. Never a day went by without some adverse publicity being splashed all over the newspapers or being aired on radio or television. Statements appeared from the chairman and others, and from the manager, and they didn't always seem to be singing from the same hymn sheet. It is no good the manager saying one thing and the chairman another. The press are quick to turn on you when things are going badly. It's great when you are winning but the situation can change very quickly. Football has a habit of kicking you up the backside just when you least expect it.

It is easy to become embroiled in the excitement when the team is doing well and Ridsdale allowed himself to do that, going out on to the pitch to sing with the fans and wave to them. Whether he allowed the fact that he was a fan to cloud his judgment, I'm not sure. He was the most approachable chairman I have ever come across. The media people I worked with could ring him at anytime and get a quote or an interview. If they had tried that with some of the other chairman in the Premiership, they wouldn't have got near to them. I think it was a genuine attempt on his part to try to be helpful to the media but his efforts earned him the nickname among some fans of 'Publicity Pete'. Sometimes you just cannot win, can you? Being aware of the value of publicity is not altogether a bad thing but in moderation because there is nothing more certain in football than that somewhere along the line the high spots are going to be replaced by low ones. When things take a turn for the worse, the press and the fans can turn on you. I found myself in that position, although on a much lower level, when I was manager at Barnsley. We had a bit of success and I used to wave to the fans but when things changed and we hit a bad patch, they quickly turned on me. Allowing yourself to be caught up in the euphoria is not the wisest thing to do.

During our Champions League campaign everyone seemed to love Leeds United and that was a real turn up for the books but in football the dividing line between success and failure can be very thin indeed. Suddenly the whole scenario can change – as it did after Leeds were denied the award of an own goal by Manchester United's Wes Brown. The points that would have given us would have meant we finished in a position to qualify for the Champions League again. Had we won that game, who knows where it would have taken us? As it was, virtually everything turned sour. We didn't just fall from grace, we hurtled to the ground and hit it with an almighty thud. The only way, it seemed, was down – and then further down.

16

FROM THE DIZZY HEIGHTS TO FINANCIAL MELTDOWN

LEEDS UNITED'S disastrous fall from grace has made the last two years a total nightmare for the club and miserable for anyone who has any feeling for the place. That's certainly true for me. It's my club. I developed a great affection for it after joining as a young trainee back in the 1960s and I've been hurt by the depths to which the club has plummeted. Let's face it, we threw money around like guests at a wedding throw confetti. The money didn't go just on players, either. It went on management, middle management and others. For me, the final straw was the sale of Jonathan Woodgate. Once we had sold him, that was it.

Peter Ridsdale's dream was to have Leeds United competing in the Champions League every season and the club's finances were geared up to that. It was a very ambitious way of looking at things – and, as things turned out for the worst, it put the club in a very precarious situation. Had it come off, it would have been fantastic but qualifying for the Champions League is a difficult job and there are no guarantees. You can make £20 million or more if you do well in Europe's major club competition and, on top of everything else that a successful club brings in from other sources, that's a major boost to finances. I think Ridsdale thought he could keep Leeds operating at that high level. He wanted to see Leeds challenging Manchester United as the top team in England and that is an admirable ambition if you have the necessary finances to back it. If you don't, it's a massive gamble. He said once that Leeds lived the dream. We did for a while, then the dream turned into a nightmare.

When things go so horribly wrong as they did at Elland Road, you instantly search for someone to take the blame and you have to look first and foremost to Ridsdale. He came in for a great deal of flak from supporters, and the media also turned on him in no uncertain manner. I didn't feel sorry for him because as chairman he was the figurehead. The supporters will, I think, always blame him for what has happened to the club but, in his defence, I must say that he could hardly have done it all on his own. It could not have been solely down to him. Other people must have been involved who should shoulder some of the blame. The board, for example, must have backed Ridsdale and, in turn, he backed the manager, David O'Leary. Gearing up for the Champions League was laudable, but when details of some of the players' contracts came out, it was a huge shock to many people. We had businessmen on the board to keep the club on a proper financial footing and most people assumed that there was some sense and logic somewhere. The club has had to pay a terrible price with the threat of administration rearing its ugly head. The people I feel sorry for most are the supporters. For many, it's not just their interest but their life. It's their club and it has been dragged into the mire.

So although O'Leary had guided Leeds to a fifth-place finish in season 2001–02 and a place in the UEFA Cup, that wasn't good enough for the board and they sacked him. With the heavy financial outlay and commitments, Leeds needed to be in the Champions League. The big gamble was about to fail.

I think O'Leary could count himself a little unfortunate to have been dismissed. He had taken the club into Europe again and I felt that the board might have stuck by him a little longer to see how his team fared in the new season. But O'Leary was out and the search was on for his successor. Again, the name of Martin O'Neill was mentioned but once more he stayed where he was. Steve McClaren at Middlesbrough was another manager linked with Leeds but in the end Ridsdale went for Terry Venables, who gave up a lucrative television contract to return to football management. I thought Venables would be good for Leeds but I'm not sure he realised fully just what he was letting himself in for. Quite a few experienced and talented players had been sold to help ease a rapidly worsening financial situation. I think he felt that he could coach his way out of trouble. He was a good coach – one of the best I have ever seen – and perhaps he thought he could get a number of players in and slot them into the Leeds side.

The writing was on the wall when Jonathan Woodgate was sold to Newcastle United for £9 million. One minute the club weren't going to sell him because, the chairman told us all, we didn't have to. The next moment they went ahead and sold him anyway. I would still like to know the ins and outs of that one, and particularly why there was the sudden change of mind. Woodgate was just one player but at that time he was vital to the team. We needed to keep hold of someone of his calibre. Venables could have built a team around him. If Woodgate had continued to develop at the same pace, I thought he had every chance of becoming as good as Rio Ferdinand, who was out-standing for Leeds – he is still one of the best central defenders I have ever seen. Can you imagine what it would have been like for Leeds if we could have had Ferdinand and Woodgate at the centre of our defence for years to come? Teams would have found it very difficult to score against us and we would have had a solid foundation on which to build.

Venables didn't have the success everyone hoped he would but he had to work under very difficult circumstances. When Leeds attempted to explain their problems and the transfer of Woodgate, the chairman and manager shared the same stage and the body language was plain for all to see. As I watched the press conference live on television, Venables looked as though he was struggling to contain his anger. So much so that I fully expected him to get up from his seat and walk out. I felt sorry for him. That press conference was ill-advised and counter-productive. It was an embarrassment because it was blatantly obvious that all was not well between the two of them. That is not the kind of thing you want to see from the two main men at the football club. Clearly the atmosphere was very strained and hardly conducive to a smooth working relationship.

In the Premiership you have to have good players to get you out of trouble and Leeds had sold a lot of theirs. Some people said Terry failed because he was a lot older than the players he had to deal with and there was too big an age gap but I don't subscribe to that view. However, I don't think he bought too well. I wouldn't have gone for Nick Barmby or Paul Okon because I didn't think they were good enough for Leeds United, but people differ in their views and that's one of the beauties of the game.

One of the biggest eye-openers to me was the way we

approached an FA Cup-tie against Sheffield United at Bramall Lane in the 2002–03 season, which we lost 1–0. The Blades had already knocked us out of the League Cup at Bramall Lane so we had the ideal opportunity to gain our revenge on them. In addition, a place in the semi-finals of the FA Cup was at stake but the team's performance that day was one of the most unbelievable and pathetic I had seen from a Leeds United side. The players just didn't perform and, what's worse, they didn't look too bothered, either. For me, that was very worrying. It must have worried Terry Venables, too. The writing was obviously on the wall for him and a couple of weeks later he was out of the club. You had to feel some sympathy for Terry because he had had the strength of his squad reduced but with Leeds having gone out of the FA Cup and sinking ever nearer to a relegation place, something had to be done and it was. Few people were surprised.

The board turned to Peter Reid as caretaker manager and his brief was simple – keep Leeds in the Premiership. But just when we thought there might be a bit of stability about the place in the final crucial weeks of the season, Peter Ridsdale resigned. Things had gone from bad to worse and the chairman's position had become untenable.

Reid had been sacked as manager of Sunderland and I imagine he jumped at the chance to get back into management, even if it was only on a short-term basis and for a Premiership club that was in a dire financial state. Professor John McKenzie came in as chairman and his job was to cut costs in the best way he could. Unfortunately, this led to redundancies among staff at the lower end of the club's pay scale. He did manage to save about £5 million or £6 million but that was a mere drop in the ocean when compared to debts of £80 million plus. It was against this unsettling backdrop that Reid had to work to save the club from dropping into the First Division. That he succeeded was due in no small measure to Mark Viduka, who conjured up some priceless goals.

We were well down the Premiership, sixteenth I think, when the burly Australian answered the call to arms and scored thirteen goals in the last nine league games of the season. None was more vital – or memorable – than the one he scored at Arsenal in the final away game of the season. Few people, if any, had given us a chance of beating Arsenal at Highbury. The Gunners were going strongly after the title and needed to beat us to remain in contention. The scores were level at 2–2 with the final minutes ticking away when Mark broke clear on the right, cut in and fired a great shot into the Gunners net. In the press box, I was up on my feet to applaud that one, unprofessional or not. It was such an important goal – it ensured our Premiership survival. Arsenal's defeat handed the championship to our old rivals Manchester United but who cared about that? I didn't. Leeds had avoided the drop and that was the main thing.

Mark has his critics, probably due to his style of play. He can look slow and cumbersome at times but that's deceptive. When he's on his game, few are better. For a big man he has exceptionally good control and skill. They say you can judge how good a player is when he's not in the side and the fact is that Leeds were not as good a side without him as they were with him.

The only thing that surprised me about Mark was why he didn't spend more time in the box. He wanted to come deep, or go down the wing. Maybe he wasn't getting much of a service from the midfield men. If that happens, a striker has to go looking for the ball. But if Mark is in the area and the ball is played in, he will get on the end of the crosses and score goals. There are not many centre-forwards – Thierry Henry and Ruud van Nistelrooy are the exceptions – who could have scored some of the outstanding goals Mark scored. I think Eddie Gray recognised his skills and made it quite obvious that if Viduka was available, he would play him. Everything went through him. With Alan Smith, who is a willing worker, alongside him, you had a good striking partnership.

Viduka's goal against Arsenal earned Reid the manager's job on a full-time basis, as well as keeping us in the Premiership. While he readily accepted it, he knew it was going to be very difficult. The club's financial plight had not improved and was as serious as it could get, far worse than I thought. I knew it was bad but when the figures were published it was outrageous. It still upsets me now to think about it. I wouldn't say it caused me sleepless nights but I was very restless. I think it was down to the fact that I knew the club was in a dreadful state and I was powerless to do anything to help. It was also hard to accept that we could sell a player and the money didn't come back to Leeds United. It went to someone else to pay off a loan fee. I never realised that was the way it worked and neither did the punters because they could not understand why, if we had debts of £80 million and we sold Rio Ferdinand for £30 million, the deficit figure didn't come down. Leeds shocked English football when they paid West Ham £18 million for Ferdinand but to get as much as they did when he was sold was good business. We lost one of our best players but just think how much higher the debts would have been had that deal not been done.

Then it turned out we were mortgaged. We'd borrowed £60

million and needed to fund that on top of everything else. Some reports put our total debt at over £100 million. How long would it have taken for such a huge debt to be paid off even if we had qualified for the Champions League? We would have had to spend further huge amounts to strengthen the team, so the debt would, in all probability, still have been there even if we had been in Europe. The situation was quite horrendous. Only a very few clubs can survive with people on the sort of salaries that Leeds paid out. That's the top and bottom of it.

To have allowed the financial situation to become as bad as it was is nothing short of scandalous. I was told that 82p in the pound went on wages and if that was the case, it was frightening. You cannot run a business like that. I know people say that football is not like an ordinary business but it should be. We wanted to finish in the top four or five and to give Manchester United a good run for their money but it proved to be a step too far for us. At one time, it looked as though Leeds could be one of the top four teams in the country. We had it within our grasp but we could not hold on to it. Now we are paying the price.

Against such an uncertain background, Peter Reid had to look ahead as best he could. In some respects, I thought he didn't have all that much luck and when you are managing a club with as many problems as Leeds had you need some good fortune. With so many players having left and with little or no money to spend on replacements, the only course of action open to Reid was to wheel and deal in the loan market. We brought in half a dozen players and signed Jody Morris on a free transfer. Jermaine Pennant's arrival from Arsenal was all to the good but some of the other loan signings were average, to say the least. We ended up with Lamine Sakho, Salomon Olembe, Zoumana Camara, Roque Junior and Didier Domi, most of whom we had never heard of. In my view, taking on as many loan players as Leeds did was a mistake, although most of them started off very brightly. Sakho, I thought, was going to set the world alight. He scored at Middlesbrough and then his confidence just went totally. Olembe went to left-back and he was better there than he was anywhere else and while Camara did all right in central defence he never looked too comfortable. Roque Junior came from AC Milan and had won a World Cup winner's medal with Brazil in 2002, but he seemed out of his depth in the Premiership. He had a fiery baptism facing up to aerial bombardment at Leicester and coming up against Duncan Ferguson at Everton. You could almost hear Duncan growling, 'Welcome to the Premier League!' I felt the physical demands were too much for Roque Junior.

Although they came without any transfer fees, we needed to pay the loan players reasonable wages. I would have thought that the amount of money that was laid out to cover those signings would have been sufficient to buy two or three good, hard-working professionals from football in England – players who were coming to the end of their careers or who could not get into the first team at their own clubs but who had experienced the Premiership or the First Division and knew what to expect. I'm thinking of Colin Cooper of Middlesbrough, who could play at the back, and then perhaps we could have found a solid midfielder. I would have preferred us to do something like that. If you believe what Reid wrote later about not being allowed to sign Patrik Berger, Paolo Di Canio, Markus Babbel or Henning Berg, you have to have some sympathy for him. They could very well have made a difference to the club.

However, we started 2003–04 better than I thought we would, losing only once in our first four games. Then we got turned over at Leicester, lost at home to Birmingham and came in for a real thumping at Everton. By the time we went to Portsmouth at the beginning of November, we had slipped to the bottom of the table. Not only were we losing matches but we were having a lot of goals scored against us, which could be very costly in the final reckoning at the end of the season. We were leaking like a sieve and a 6–1 defeat at Fratton Park proved to be the final blow for Reid.

As the goals went in with such regularity at Portsmouth, I think Reid must have known he was for the chop. He is a nice enough bloke but, being Reid, he fell out with Viduka. That was probably the wrong thing to do at the time because Leeds needed all the players they could get and especially the big-name players, which Viduka undoubtedly is. Personally, I don't think Leeds could have carried on with Reid. I think he had to go. Although I probably wouldn't have given him the job in the first place, I don't think it would have mattered who had come in because, to a great extent, their hands would have been tied. There was no money to spend on players.

It was essential that Leeds appointed someone to replace Reid as quickly as possible and I could think of no one better than Eddie Gray. I personally believe that Eddie had a point to prove. He had been the manager and the coach previously and in his last job with Leeds he had been assistant manager, a post from which he was made redundant after Reid came in. When Eddie returned, he brought a great attitude to the job. Like me, he has the club at heart and when I spoke to him shortly after he took over, he told me he was really enjoying the job, although how he could have been enjoying it under such difficult circumstances was beyond me. He genuinely loves the club, the players and football in general, and for the difficult period the club found themselves in, he was the right man to turn to. He had everything that the club needed – enthusiasm, a great knowledge of the game and coaching skills, even though he doesn't have the little bits of paper that say he is a qualified coach. He's steeped in the game and in Leeds United.

I have heard it said that Eddie is too soft but that's nonsense. He's an extremely nice person but he knows his mind and there is no way you will ever win an argument with him. He has a caring attitude, the fans love him and the players responded to him and to coach Kevin Blackwell, who is very highly qualified.

It was good to see Eddie back at the club. I still think Leeds treated him badly in the 1980s after he had taken over as manager from Allan Clarke, with the club in the Second Division. Eddie was at Leeds for over three years and he did a good job at a difficult time and there were a lot of people who didn't agree with the decision to sack him in 1985. I wasn't surprised, though, that he fancied another crack at it.

Eddie faced an enormous task to keep Leeds in the top flight but, in many ways, he was going to be blameless whatever the final outcome. No one could blame him for the managerial situation or the financial state of the club or the failures on the field before he took over – and if he had been able to save the club from relegation, he would have been a hero and, for my money, manager of the season.

I was dreading the re-opening of the transfer window at the beginning of January because I honestly thought we would lose one or two of our top players. I was hoping against hope that we could hold on to them because, frankly, if that hadn't been the case, it would have signalled the end for us as a Premiership club there and then. Alan Smith, Paul Robinson, Mark Viduka, even young James Milner, were all targeted by other clubs and the indications seemed to be that one or two of those players would be on their way out of Elland Road. It was vital to us that Viduka didn't go anywhere and I was very relieved that we managed to keep him, despite Middlesbrough's strong interest. I thought it was a good thing, too, that Paul Robinson didn't go to Tottenham. I know the financial situation was as bad as it could be but we needed to hold on to our best players if we were to have any chance at all of avoiding the dreaded drop. In the end, though, we failed.

It was a pity that Viduka had to go back to Australia to be with his seriously ill father but some things are more important than football and I don't see how the club could have done anything other than allow Mark some compassionate leave to be at his father's bedside. When Mark returned to Leeds he was in a very positive mood and I was very impressed with his attitude. He threw in his lot with Leeds and showed great commitment. I liked what he was doing and I thought his reactions in the 4–1 home win over Wolves in February underlined his strong feeling for the survival fight. When the final whistle went, and when anybody scored, he was the first to celebrate, jumping around everybody, and he also scored himself. He got other players psyched up. I think that Eddie told Mark and Alan Smith before the Wolves game that if anyone could save the club from relegation, it was them.

Apart from the three points, the thing that struck me about the victory was the manner in which Leeds won it. The first two goals were scrappy and very ordinary but it was the attitude and the way the team worked that impressed me. Leeds chased and harried and put Wolves under pressure. Both Viduka and Smith, especially Smith, occupied the Wolves central defenders, and that was the first time we had seen that all season. They did not allow the defenders any rest. Smith won headers, Viduka got flicks, Jermaine Pennant and James Milner moved well on the wings and cut inside. Eirik Bakke didn't go beyond the ball but played behind it and our two central defenders looked fairly sound. All of a sudden, players were prepared to stand up and be counted and for the first time in months I felt we had a chance of avoiding the drop. A draw at Manchester United in the next game followed by a home draw against Liverpool gave me further confidence that the players were capable of keeping Leeds in the Premier League.

At last, the long-suffering but very patient fans had some hope to cling on to, something to suggest the club was not doomed after all. All fans ask is for players to give 100 per cent every time they go out on the pitch. I found it amazing that there was the need, seemingly, to say to players that they had to go out and work hard. If you are a player and you are not playing well, the natural thing to do is work hard, and if you do that, the fans notice it and accept the situation much better. There is no finer example than Alan Smith. His goalscoring record may not be quite what it should be for a player of his ability but he gives everything he has. He works his socks off every time he plays and the fans adore him for that.

17

DOOM AND GLOOM
. . . BUT THERE'S
ALWAYS HOPE

I NEVER thought I would say this but I really hated going to watch Leeds United play in 2003–04. It was not so much the type of football they played – which was hardly the best – but the gut feeling I had that they were more likely to lose matches than win them and the fear that they were not good enough to pull things around. To me, there seemed to be an air of inevitability about the season – we were heading for the drop. In the final analysis those fears were realised but I have to admit that we got what we deserved. We weren't good enough to survive in the Premiership and we didn't.

It wasn't a pleasant experience. In fact, the past year or two have slowly torn me apart. The club I love has been dragged through the mud. I was going to matches hoping and praying that we might make some headway but most of the time my prayers went unanswered. Match after match, I witnessed Leeds tumbling to disaster and it was all the more painful because I knew that I was powerless to do anything about it. It was my worst football experience since joining the club as an apprentice in 1960.

The final six or seven weeks of the 2003–04 campaign were absolutely horrendous. I had lost all my enthusiasm for the game and it was a toil to go to matches. Football – and Leeds United – has been a massive part of my life but I found I was going to games just because I was contracted to attend them in my role as a radio summariser. Had that not been the case, I don't think I would have gone to a lot of the matches.

Not all that long ago I would drive to games full of enthusiasm, knowing that I would enjoy them. We would have a laugh and a bit of banter and we would see some good football. That was when we had Harry Kewell, Jonathan Woodgate, Lee Bowyer, Rio Ferdinand, Nigel Martyn and Olivier Dacourt as well as Alan Smith and Mark Viduka. It didn't matter whom we were playing – Manchester United, Liverpool, Arsenal, anyone, in fact – I would be thinking we could win the game. There was never any thought about losing. We had a very good side that was capable of beating any team on its day.

Sadly, the opposite was the case in 2003–04. Having been a player, it is hard to sit there and watch things go wrong. I took defeats personally and as badly as when I was a player. I just couldn't help it. People would say to me that it was not my living and that it had nothing to do with me any more but that wasn't how I looked at it. What was happening was happening to my club.

The support Leeds received during the bad times was nothing short of amazing. Despite the disappointments and problems, they turned up in their thousands week in and week out and stayed right to the bitter end to support the club and, let's face it, at times they had the biggest load of rubbish to watch.

When you are struggling as a team, you really need the support of the fans and not every club gets that once things start going wrong. I just couldn't believe how supportive the Leeds fans were. When I was a player the fans were very quick to moan and I have to admit that I thought they would do the same now but instead they did their best to encourage the players when things got really bad. It wasn't always the team's fault because so many top-class players had been sold. You can have the best motivators and coaches in the world but if you don't have players as good as, or better than, the opposition, you are going to struggle.

It was all so very different when we were flying high in the Premiership and the Champions League and everyone wanted to know about the club for all the right reasons. I would breeze into press rooms at various grounds full of the joys of spring, so to speak. The minute I walked in someone was up and over to me, eager to talk about the Leeds United team. When Leeds were doing well under David O'Leary I went to matches not hoping but expecting Leeds would win, such was the ability and confidence in the side. During the relegation season I walked into press rooms hoping people would not ask me about the Leeds team because it depressed me to talk about it.

When the final whistle blew at Stamford Bridge on the last day of the season to signal the end of our fourteen-year stay in the top flight of football, the realisation that Leeds United had been relegated left me with an empty feeling in my stomach. The fact that a new board had managed to save the club from administration, and very likely liquidation, a couple of months earlier had little effect on the dejection I felt at having seen my club lose its Premier League status.

I think many supporters had expected the worst to happen

and the club to be relegated, but at the same time, we had retained a slim hope that the odds that were so heavily stacked against Leeds could be overcome. It was a forlorn hope at the best of times yet when relegation was finally confirmed, it still came as a big shock. Usually, I am an avid viewer of the Saturday night football highlights on television but I could count on the fingers of one hand how many times I switched on ITV's 'The Premiership' programme that season. Watching Leeds lose matches – and quite a few by a big margin – is not my idea of good late-night viewing, and having attended the games, I had no real desire to watch them again.

The press had it in for us and feasted on the continuing problems, particularly those concerned with finances and the club's fight to stay in existence. At one stage, I think we got as much space on the financial pages as we did on the sports pages. We had more than our fair share of front pages, too. The players took a lot of stick from the press and while some of it was justified, I thought it was disgraceful that the newspapers printed what individual players at the club were earning and which players were allegedly refusing to defer some of their wages when the financial situation at the club got so bad that administration became a real possibility. Things like that should remain private. It seemed the papers were trying to alienate the players from the fans and that was shocking.

Some of the salaries that were published were astronomical, though – frightening really. Paying wages of £1 million, £1.5 million, £2 million and as much as £3 million a year is ridiculous.

I don't think there would have been any dissent if the Leeds players I played with had been asked to defer some of their wages. We weren't on anything like the vast sums that players are paid today but if I had been on £30,000 or £40,000 a week and had been asked to defer, I would have agreed for the sake of the club. You talk it over with your wife first and foremost but, faced with that kind of situation, there would have been no danger of the players of my era not agreeing to a deferral, even on the wages they received.

The request was a desperate last resort. Overall, if you look at what the club were asking of the players, it was not as if they would lose any money. It had to be a unanimous thing. You couldn't expect some players to do it while others collected their full pay. That would have split the players totally and utterly down the middle. I hoped they would agree, if only for the sake of the long-suffering supporters, and in the end the players did the honourable thing, agreed to the wage deferral and the club was able to carry on long enough for an agreement to be reached with new buyers.

I first started not to enjoy games when Terry Venables was manager and it continued under Peter Reid. When Eddie Gray took over he did manage to steady the ship for a while, but it was an enormous task. The game against Wolves in February gave us hope but the crunch game came at the beginning of May, against Bolton, when Leeds were effectively relegated. I didn't see it but I saw Eddie's face on television afterwards and I felt dreadfully sorry for him. You could see the hurt he felt but you couldn't blame him for Leeds' failure to retain their Premiership status. The odds were always stacked against him.

We did have a short spell – five games unbeaten – when we looked as though we might be able to survive in the Premier League, but the other teams that were fighting against relegation managed to raise their game. Portsmouth, for instance, went on a great run, Middlesbrough pulled out of it and so did Everton, Blackburn Rovers and Manchester City. When the going got really tough, we were found wanting. We managed to beat Blackburn and Leicester in back-to-back games but other than that we fell woefully short and paid a heavy price. Our plight wasn't helped when Mark Viduka got himself sent off twice in the vital run-in. His actions let the side down because, in my opinion, both dismissals were unnecessary.

Once our fate was decided I actually felt relieved. I was gutted at seeing Leeds out of the top flight but I had been put out of my misery. What we always feared had become a reality. We had been hanging on to every little hope that we might pull it off but we didn't and at least we knew where we were. We just weren't good enough. Defensively, we had an appalling record. We were very, very weak. Goals were going in left, right and centre. We couldn't stop anything at vital times and you could sense we were always vulnerable. When you let in 79 goals, as we did in the Premiership, you have to ask serious questions about the defenders. It doesn't take a genius to know that there needs to be some drastic reconstruction there. We also had injuries to midfield players, which meant Eddie had to use central defenders in midfield and as a result we didn't have much creativity. In turn, this meant that the forwards were not getting the kind of service they needed. We had so few players that we had to make do and mend. I think most of the players gave everything they could for Eddie but if you're slightly inferior, especially in the Premiership, you've not much chance. The league table tells you everything. It doesn't lie. We were one of the worst teams in the Premiership.

I was very disappointed when the club decided to relieve Eddie of the managerial duties. You won't find anyone with a better knowledge of the game or with greater enthusiasm for Leeds United than Eddie. I was pleased to see that he would be staying on at the club as a consultant. The new manager, Kevin Blackwell, who was Eddie's chief coach, will have his own ideas, of course, though with Peter Lorimer at the club as a director and Eddie as consultant he will have two very knowledgeable people to turn to should he want any advice.

But now that he is manager he will be his own man. When you are in the managerial hot-seat you need to be strong and decisive and, having been at Sheffield United before he moved to Elland Road, he will also have a good knowledge of the First Division, which I think will be important. The financial restraints at Leeds will make a difficult job all the harder and I wish him well.

There is so much to be done. Inevitably, relegation means you lose most of your better players. That is a fact of footballing life. Those sales generate much-needed cash and you then have the vital task of trying to bring in new players who will blend in with the young players who are at the club.

It was vitally important that the board made the right decision in selecting the new manager – so much rests on his shoulders. The departure of Alan Smith and Mark Viduka left Leeds without any recognised striker so one if not two new forwards were needed. The five loan players in the squad left, too, while goalkeeper Paul Robinson was transferred to Tottenham and a lot of team rebuilding had to be undertaken, with not all that long to do it in. Without much cash available to spend on players, Kevin Blackwell has to be spot on when he does buy. He cannot afford to make any misjudgements.

Smith was an immensely popular player at Leeds but even he

must have been surprised at the way the fans reacted to him at the end of the last home game. They came on to the pitch in their hundreds to bid farewell to the home-town boy. I had never seen scenes like that before. I would have hated it but, judging by his smiling face, he loved it. Smithy was passionate about playing football for Leeds and I like him as an individual, but he needs to score more goals than he has done. He is at the stage of his career now where he needs to play alongside a good and experienced striker, and learn from him. It will be interesting to see how he gets on at Old Trafford. He might also benefit by being a little bit more selfish and playing in the penalty box more. There is no doubt that if he can score more regularly, he will be a really tremendous player and a great asset to any club.

The road ahead for Leeds is a difficult one. There are a few very good sides in the First Division, better than Leeds in 2003–04, so there are bound to be problems ahead as the club rebuilds virtually from scratch. Eddie Gray would have been ideal at bringing along younger players, which is what the aim must be. If Leeds can do what West Bromwich Albion did and come straight back to the Premier League, relegation will have been a good thing. Leeds could not have sustained the kind of wages they were paying out and if promotion can be achieved without those high earners, the club will be on a much better footing. I know that's a big 'if' and the indications are that it will take longer than one season to re-establish Leeds United as a force in English football. I think the club will have to adopt a long-term plan. When you think what has gone on in the past four years, it is likely to take some time for the club to recover and get back to where it was. There is no short-term fix. We have to avoid the mistakes that were made last time. The long-term future of the club is important and producing players through the academy has to be the way forward.

When we were in the Champions League three years ago, I never for one moment thought the club would be relegated. Once we started the downward spiral – and I thought the beginning of the end was the transfer of Jonathan Woodgate to Newcastle United – we went downhill at a very rapid rate. We lost too many high-profile players and no club in any footballing country could have coped with that. We sold half a team and you just cannot do that. Football is an unpredictable business and most clubs take risks in the quest for success but, as Leeds found out, that can have catastrophic repercussions. Although we were high flyers in the transfer market, it was felt that, should things go wrong, we could always make a profit by selling players. Unfortunately, the bottom fell out of the transfer market and it cost us dear.

Peter Ridsdale's dream was for Leeds United to compete in the Champions League every season and we gambled accordingly. It was an ambitious way of looking at things and, as things turned out, it put the club in a precarious situation. The last-minute takeover by Gerald Krasner's consortium saved the club from possible extinction. It would be unthinkable for a city the size of Leeds to be without a professional football club.

After the season officially ended with that 1–0 defeat at Chelsea, I couldn't help but think about the situations of both clubs. Just a year earlier Chelsea, like Leeds, had been in dire financial straits with crippling debts hung around their neck. When the two clubs met at Stamford Bridge on the final day of the 2003–04 campaign, there could hardly have been a greater turnaround in fortunes. Roman Abramovich's many millions had bailed Chelsea out in

the nick of time while Leeds, in the absence of any such bene-
factor, were left to fend for themselves and battle on under the
weight of enormous difficulties.

On the journey back to Leeds from Chelsea, I confessed to
my travelling companion that I had lost all interest in the game.
'I'm fed up with football,' I told him.

I'll get over it. I'll be back and raring to go next season. That's
the way it is with football. When it's in your blood, as it has been
in mine for as long as I can remember, there is always hope . . .

INDEX